Teaching at the People's University

Teaching at the People's University

An Introduction to the State Comprehensive University

Bruce B. Henderson
Western Carolina University

Anker Publishing Company, Inc.
Bolton, Massachusetts

Teaching at the People's University
An Introduction to the State Comprehensive University

ISBN 978-1-933371-10-8

Composition by Tanya Anoush Johnson, Senior Designer
Cover design by Rebecca Krzyzaniak

Anker Publishing Company, Inc.
563 Main Street
P.O. Box 249
Bolton, MA 01740-0249 USA

www.ankerpub.com

Library of Congress Cataloging-in-Publication Data
Henderson, Bruce B., 1950-
    Teaching at the people's university : an introduction to the state comprehensive university / Bruce B. Henderson.
        p. cm.
Includes bibliographical references and index.
    ISBN-13: 978-1-933371-10-8
    1. Public universities and colleges—United States.
    2. Public universities and colleges—United States—Faculty.
    I. Title.

    LB2328.62.U6H46 2007
    378.050973—dc22

                                              2006015745

To my family

Table of Contents

About the Author

Bruce B. Henderson is professor of psychology at Western Carolina University. He has bachelor's and master's degrees in psychology from Bucknell University and a doctorate in child psychology from the University of Minnesota's Institute of Child Development. He has received the Botner Superior Teaching Award and the University of North Carolina Board of Governors Award for Excellence in Teaching and is a Fellow of the American Psychological Association. Most of his publications have focused on the development of children's curiosity, memory development, or ways to improve teaching. He participated in the American Psychological Association's St. Mary's Conference on Undergraduate Education and Alverno College's Critical Thinking Network. The Spencer Foundation and the Foundation for Child Development are among the sources that have supported his research. He has worked on a variety of research and training projects with the University of Houston, Northern Kentucky University, the Yale University Child Study Center, the North Carolina Center for the Advancement of Teaching, and the University of North Carolina–Chapel Hill.

Preface

The higher education landscape has changed a great deal over the past 50 years and will surely continue to change. Some scholars of higher education believe that universities are looking more and more alike as lower status institutions slavishly copy the higher status ones. In this view, rather than trying to respond to distinctive missions, universities of humble origins try to emulate the prestigious research universities and move up a Carnegie class or two. Faculty members also seek status by lobbying for low teaching loads so they will have more time for their scholarly work. Other scholars of higher education see a growing diversity within higher education as state colleges and universities respond to the economic needs of their tax-paying constituencies, small colleges become more customer oriented, and the traditional elites become even more elitist. The 2005 revision of the Carnegie classification attempts to put some order to the chaos of diversity that the old system could not describe.

As usual the truth is probably somewhere in the middle of these two views. I suspect faculty members see the first perspective as more accurate while administrators, trustees, and legislators see the second as more accurate and more desirable. What both views share is the recognition that higher education will continue to change. I would add that even if those who hold various views do not realize it, at least some of that change will be largely unpredictable. This state of flux might raise questions about the usefulness of a book that tries to describe a segment of higher education as it is in the early 21st century. However, I offer this introduction to state comprehensive universities in the belief that there are some stable features in the flux, at least for the foreseeable future. These stable features include:

1) Research universities will continue to prepare most of the faculty members for all types of colleges and universities by emphasizing training in disciplinary research.

2) State comprehensive universities (in whatever form they take) will attempt to educate many students who come to college with a wide range of abilities, skills, and motivation with the expectation that they will be prepared for the world of work.

3) At state comprehensive universities, conducting traditional research will be a less important role for faculty members than the ability to effectively teach students with diverse degrees of preparation and, at most comprehensive universities, less important than the ability to provide meaningful educational services to local regions.

4) The combination of features 1–3 means that faculty members hired by state comprehensive universities will:
   • Often struggle with role conflict engendered by expectations for involvement in research as modeled in their graduate training
   • Sometimes experience the loss of the prestige and status (along with more tangible rewards) bestowed on those who do most of the research in American higher education

I wrote this book to introduce new and aspiring faculty members to the state comprehensive university and what it is like to be a faculty member there. I believe many new faculty members at comprehensive universities have a misleading set of assumptions about academic life. Those assumptions and subsequent role conflicts come with them from their graduate training at the research university, from general ideas about what universities are like, and from stereotypes about college professors. Some of these assumptions about academic life do not correspond well with the realities of the modern public comprehensive university. The new faculty member can recognize the discrepancies or not and can adapt to the realities of the comprehensive university or not. I believe those faculty members who, first, recognize the differences between working at a comprehensive university and working at a research university or liberal arts college and, second, are willing to adapt to those differences, are most likely to have careers that they find rewarding and that benefit their students and institutions. Moreover, unless faculty members understand the role of comprehensive universities in higher education, they are not likely to take pride in their institutions or in their jobs. I am convinced there are major advantages to the academic life of the public comprehensive university and hope to convince you I am right. I have spent almost 30 years at a public comprehensive university after being educated at a liberal arts college and a major research university. Early in my career I sometimes struggled with understanding my milieu. I would like to help others come to that understanding more quickly and easily.

I wrote this book while on a study leave provided by Western Carolina University. The staff at Hunter Library was very helpful in many ways during that period. Many colleagues have helped me formulate the ideas in this book and have helped me express those ideas better. Carol Burton, Heidi Buchanan, Robert Henderson, Anna MacFadden, and Bill Kane all provided much useful feedback on earlier drafts. Bill Kane helped me formulate many of the ideas that have been developed in this book through years of thoughtful discussion. They all deserve most of the blame if you do not like this book.

1 Introduction: Distinctive Features of the State Comprehensive University

In her presidential address to the Association for the Study of Higher Education (ASHE), Austin (2002) summarized the internal and external changes in higher education and its social and political milieu that were having a direct impact on the work and lives of faculty members. She argued that new expectations require that the next generation of faculty members acquire knowledge and skills different from those obtained by previous generations. Aspiring and new faculty members currently do not understand how different types of institutions vary in mission, student characteristics, institutional cultures, and expectations for faculty performance. Many new faculty members will be entering the profession in the coming decade. Few will find jobs in the research sector in which they are receiving their graduate training. Austin called for major changes in the preparation of new faculty members to help them succeed in the nonresearch institutions.

One of the most common types of institution, perhaps the most common (Nerad & Cerny, 1999), where aspiring faculty members will find jobs is the state comprehensive university. In this introductory chapter, I provide an overview of the basic nature of the state comprehensive university, its distinctive features, and

1

some of the special problems faced by faculty members there. I then briefly describe the chapters of the book and how they deal with the special problems.

What Is a State Comprehensive University?

The state comprehensive university is part of an American higher education system that includes more than 3,000 colleges and universities. Classifying those institutions in a meaningful way is a difficult task. The Carnegie Foundation for the Advancement of Teaching started categorizing institutions in 1971. Then and in subsequent Carnegie categorizations in 1976, 1987, 1994, and 2000, the categories were mutually exclusive. The 2005 version of the Carnegie classes is much more complex, combining several different ways of classifying institutions, reflecting the difficulty of finding useful ways to sort out similarities and differences among institutions (McCormick & Zhao, 2005). Despite the difficulties of classifying colleges and universities, across the various Carnegie versions there has been a category that includes the state comprehensive universities that has been relatively stable. In earlier versions the category was called *public comprehensive universities* while in the later versions it has been *public master's institutions* (in each case the colleges and universities in the category were sorted into two classes, I and II, with distinctions made between larger schools with more graduate programs and smaller ones with fewer programs).

In this book I use the term *state comprehensive university* (SCU) because I think it is more descriptive than *master's institution*. The name of the category provides a rough idea what a state comprehensive university is. The state part is obvious. The bulk of the funding for SCUs comes from state government, although as in other state-funded colleges there has been a recent shift of funding toward student-provided tuition and fees. The term *comprehensive* is used in contrast to *single purpose* or *limited purpose*. Many of the SCUs started as single-purpose teacher training institutions or agricultural training schools (see Chapter 2). Over the course of the 20th century, their curricula expanded to include dozens of different kinds of programs in every academic discipline. They became more comprehensive. Finally, they are called universities because most SCUs have for some time awarded master's degrees, and some also offer doctorates in a limited number of fields.

The Carnegie classes are fluid, in part because they have come to represent a status hierarchy and some institutions are always trying to move up the hierarchy. Perhaps a good operational definition of the SCUs as a category is that they are institutions in the current Carnegie classes of Master's I and Master's II universities. The SCUs also overlap to a large degree with the membership of the American Association of State Colleges and Universities (AASCU). However, AASCU includes a number of members who are in the Carnegie classification of doctoral institutions. Many of these institutions have significantly changed their missions in recent decades and have been described as research university wannabes. They have often changed their identities and missions in fundamental ways that make them unlike the SCUs.

It is difficult to report the precise number of students at SCUs at any one time. It is clear that a very large portion of students in four-year colleges and universities are enrolled at SCUs. For the year 2000, the U.S. Department of Education National Center for Education Statistics (NCES; 2003) listed 2,286,819 students in 275 public master's institutions. In comparison, 4,122,168 students attended 166 public doctoral institutions and 327,599 attended 100 baccalaureate institutions. In 2000 more than 55% of the students enrolled in four-year public colleges and universities were in AASCU colleges and universities. According to AASCU (2002), 3.45 million students were at AASCU-member schools in 2000. No matter how the numbers are computed, SCUs are a major force in American higher education. Despite their important role, SCUs have received remarkably little attention from scholars: "The research and writing on these institutions is exceedingly sparse" (Grubb & Lazerson, 2005, p. 20). This book provides an overview of what research and writing do exist.

Distinctive Features of the SCU

In many ways American four-year colleges and universities are more alike than they are different. The obvious features of a modern university are present at schools at all levels, including SCUs. Common features include physical features such as laboratories and gymnasiums, fiscal features such as tuition and fees, curricular features such as general education and majors, and personnel features such as students, faculty members, staff, and administrators. However, I argue that there are significant enough differences to make academic life different at SCUs. What are the features of the SCUs that make working in them different? In Table 1 I have compared

SCUs to research universities, baccalaureate colleges, and community colleges. For simplicity, I focus on what the Carnegie system identifies as Baccalaureate–Liberal Arts schools. The Baccalaureate–General category includes a very diverse group of mostly very small, often poorly funded schools.

Size

Although there are exceptions, most research universities, public or private, are very large (40,000 students and larger). Liberal arts colleges tend to be small. Community colleges vary greatly from small to as large as any research university. Although there is great diversity in size at SCUs, most are in the middle size range, from 3,000 to 15,000 students. Overall, size is not a very effective discriminator. Average class sizes at liberal arts colleges and community colleges are generally small in comparison to some of the very large undergraduate courses at major universities (in contrast to very small class sizes in their doctoral programs). SCUs tend to be in the middle, with most classes relatively small, but with considerable variability.

Funding

Public research universities, community colleges, and SCUs are funded by taxpayers, supplemented by tuition and fees that have been low historically. Liberal arts colleges and some smaller private research universities (including many of the most elite) rely on tuition and endowments. Major research universities rely much more than SCUs on research grants. Tuition and fees tend to be higher at SCUs than at community colleges, but historically have been much lower than those at private

6   *Teaching at the People's University*

Table 1.1.
Comparative Features of SCUs and Other Institutional Types

Feature	SCUs	Research/ Doctoral	Liberal Arts	Community College
Size	Medium– Large	Very large	Small	Small– Very large
Funding	State, Tuition	State, Tuition, Research, Endowment	Tuition, Endowment	State, Tuition
Selectivity & Retention	Low–Moderate	Moderate– High	High	Low
Mission	Regional focus, Vocational	Nation, Global focus, Professional	Student focus, Liberal	Local focus, Vocational
Graduate Education	Master's, Specialist	Doctoral, Professional	Limited or None	None
Research/ Teaching Emphasis	Teaching	Research	Teaching	Teaching
Athletics	Moderate, DI, DII	Major, DI	DIII	None to Minor
Carnegie Class	Master's	Doctoral/ Research	Baccalaureate	Associates

Size: small < 2,500 students; medium ≈ 2,500–10,000 students; large ≈ 10,001–20,000 students; very large > 20,000 students

Selectivity: high < 50% of applicants accepted; moderate ≈ 51–75% of applicants accepted; low > 75% of applicants accepted

schools. Although the trend has been toward higher reliance on tuition and less on direct funding, that difference still holds.

Selection and Retention of Students

Selectivity usually depends on some combination of test scores (SAT or ACT) and high school grades and/or rank. Some of the baccalaureate institutions (the elite liberal arts colleges) tend to be the most selective, followed by major research universities. Community colleges tend to have open admissions policies. SCUs are in the middle. Their students tend to be less well prepared than those at research universities or elite liberal arts colleges, but better prepared than most community college students, particularly the traditional-age students. Retention and graduation rates are often low at SCUs. In part those low rates are due to a critical characteristic of the SCUs throughout their histories: an emphasis on access. They have provided educational opportunities for students from all racial, ethnic, and social-class groups (Dunham, 1969; see Bardo, 1990). Many SCUs have created honors colleges that enroll select groups of students with lures of small classes and special programming that result in much higher retention and graduation rates. Major research universities, public and private, and most elite liberal arts schools tend to serve students from a wider geographical area than do SCUs.

Mission

The major aspect of mission that historically differentiated SCUs from other four-year universities was the emphasis on applied curricula, applied service, and applied research. Many SCUs started as teacher training institutions and have always included many curricula that prepared students for jobs. Although a balance must be struck between pure vocational training for particular jobs and a broader form of education that gives students a set of generalizable, adaptable skills in the context of preparation for work (Giroux, 1999), most students at SCUs are going directly to some kind of job, not to graduate school (although graduate enrollment often comes later). Graduates of SCUs typically are headed for middle-level managerial or service positions (Grubb & Lazerson, 2005).

The distinctiveness of the SCUs in regard to an applied emphasis has decreased in recent years. Throughout higher education there has been a growing trend toward vocationalism (Brint, Riddle, Turk-Bicakci, & Levy, 2005; Grubb & Lazerson, 2005). Grubb and Lazerson (2005) argue that the general cultural trend in America toward vocationalism led to the expansion of the SCUs (referred to by them as "second-tier" universities). In Pace and Connolly's (2000) study of majors in the liberal arts from 1983 to 1998, the relative enrollment in basic disciplines stayed the same in comprehensive universities and even went up at doctoral institutions, but significantly decreased at elite liberal arts schools.

Most SCUs are known as *regional*, not only because they tend to serve students from a particular region, but because their students and staffs are engaged in a wide array of economic and cultural activities in their areas (e.g., consulting to businesses and schools, leadership for economic development). Research universities have more national and international constituencies for their research and services.

Graduate Education

Closely related to mission is the relative emphasis on graduate versus undergraduate programs. Community colleges do not have graduate programs, and liberal arts colleges usually have few or none. SCUs tend to emphasize masters programs in applied fields, especially education and business, but increasingly in technology and the health sciences. SCUs typically do not offer doctorates in the sciences, social sciences, or humanities.

Research and Teaching Emphasis

The core activity for research institutions is research. Faculty members are judged by their ability to publish research and obtain external funding. The core activity of the other kinds of institutions is teaching. As I will argue in the chapter on research, there has been a good deal of rhetoric at the SCUs about a growing emphasis on emulating research universities, but teaching remains the most important function. SCU faculty members spend less time on research and more in direct contact with students than those at research universities. They also have higher teaching loads and fewer research facilities.

Athletics

Athletics programs are almost always important at research universities. They are used as prestige generators. Most liberal arts colleges keep athletics at modest levels. SCUs are in the middle. Some play NCAA Division I sports except for football where Division IAA is more common. Many others have kept their sports participation at the Division II level. Regardless, for SCUs, sport is only rarely a prestige generator at more than a local level (the most common exception is occasional participation in the NCAA basketball tournament).

The distinctive profile presented by SCUs is apparent from the entries in Table 1.1. SCUs are not traditional liberal arts colleges nor are they major research universities. SCUs have often been called the middle child of higher education. In many ways that description is apt.

Greedy Institutions?

The middleness of SCUs presents special problems for their faculty members. Socialized in the research model, but working in settings with relatively heavy teaching and service loads, faculty members face conflicting demands, many self-imposed. Coser (1974) coined the term *greedy institutions* to describe formal organizations that place high demands on employees. Greedy institutions want both time and loyalty from their members. Sociologists Wright et al. (2004) applied the concept of greedy institutions to postsecondary education. They argue that the term fits colleges and universities, because they demand that so many different roles be filled, including teaching, publishing, getting grants, advising, and service to the community, institution, and discipline. Wright et al. categorized colleges and universities into three types: teaching oriented, research oriented, and comprehensive. Liberal arts colleges fit the first category, research universities the second, and public and private comprehensives the third. In their analysis, Wright et al. conclude that while all colleges and universities tend to be greedy, comprehensive universities are the greediest of all, because they want the teaching emphasis of the liberal arts college combined with the emphasis on research of the major university, although at lower levels.

Greedy may or may not be the best way to describe the problem, but there is evidence that the multiple demands on faculty members at SCUs engender role conflict. Indirect evidence comes from studies of academic life that show that faculty members at SCUs are less happy with their jobs than are those in other academic settings. Baldridge, Curtis, Ecker, and Riley

(1978), in their study of faculty members from different types of institutions, found that satisfaction was lower at comprehensive universities than it was at any other kind of four-year institution. Similar results were reported by Bowen and Schuster (1986) and Russell et al. (1990).

There also is evidence that the early part of the academic career is particularly stressful for faculty members at comprehensive universities. Perry, Menec, Struthers, Hechter, Schonwetter, and Menges (1997) followed new faculty members at different types of institutions over a three year period. For analysis, they combined comprehensive and liberal arts faculty members together and compared them to those from research universities (Carnegie Research I) and community colleges. The rationale for combining the comprehensives and the liberal arts colleges was that faculty members in both types of institutions have multiple expectations, whereas faculty members at the research universities were clearly focused on research, and those at the community colleges focused on teaching. According to Perry et al., a logical prediction would be that those in the comprehensive–liberal arts group would be most satisfied. They have the best of all worlds with jobs that combine research and teaching. Perry et al.'s findings about the adjustment of new hires were clear. Faculty members in the comprehensive–liberal arts group had the most difficult adjustment in their early careers (and it worsened over the three years). Perry et al. concluded that the multiple roles put excessive pressure on the new hires. Faculty members in the research universities and those in the community colleges, the institutions with more focused missions, adjusted better (and about equally well).

A report from a consortium of higher education organizations (Adams, 2002) indicates problems in the preparation of prospective faculty members for most of the academic jobs that are available. Adams summarizes research that documents a mismatch between the nature of graduate school preparation and the tasks involved in faculty positions outside the research university. Faculty members at research universities do not provide the information or experiences to their graduate students that would allow them to learn about working in nonresearch settings. Graduate students get mixed messages about the importance of teaching and receive little help in learning how to teach effectively (see Wulff, Austin, Nyquist, & Sprague, 2004). They learn nothing about advising students. Graduate students are not prepared to do research under conditions in which time is limited and facilities are even more limited. Adams's report calls for graduate programs to do a much better job preparing their students for the realities of academic lives in a wide variety of types of institutions. Similar arguments have been made by others (e.g., Pruitt-Logan & Gaff, 2004).

Conclusion and Preview

SCUs have often been their own worst enemies. Sometimes they have pandered to unprepared students, employed unprepared faculty members, sold their souls to the sports machine, overextended their curriculum and their faculties, caved to the gods of status and prestige, failed to challenge their students, and encouraged worthless, even silly, research. Yet the SCUs are underappreciated. As you will see in the chapters that follow, the SCUs democratized and continue to democratize higher education. At their best, SCUs focus on student learning in dedicated and frequently innovative ways, engage in useful service with their local communities, and offer students and their families an affordable alternative to flagship universities and private colleges. SCUs are doing good work.

The term *people's college* was long associated with land-grant colleges. But for a long while, land-grant universities have emulated the research university model, often downplaying their community outreach and increasing their admissions criteria, reducing access. Herbst (1989) has argued that it was normal schools, the ancestors of so many of the SCUs, that were the real people's colleges. They were the schools that democratized education in much of our country. I agree with Herbst. I also believe that teaching at SCUs is distinctively different from teaching in other situations and it should be. Those who work in the comprehensive university sector trade an emphasis on prestige and selectivity for the opportunity to teach a wider group, serve their communities, and conduct modest amounts of research, largely free of many of the constraints of external funding or the impositions of the disciplines.

In this book I introduce the newcomer to the state comprehensive university and how working there is similar and different from working at other institutions of higher education. This is not a how-to book. There are plenty of those, some of which I refer to later in terms of how helpful they are to faculty members at SCUs (see the Appendix). My aim is to act as a guide to a new culture. I want the newcomer to the SCU to get a conceptual overview that will provide understanding and appreciation of the advantages of teaching at SCUs (Vanderstaay, 2005). In Chapter 2 I provide a brief history of the SCUs. I focus on the SCUs that came from the normal schools and teachers colleges, because so many have had that history, and also because it is that history that has arguably colored the academic culture throughout the SCU category. In Chapter 3 I address the central issue that seems to plague individuals at SCUs and the institutions themselves: the problem of status. I argue that SCUs and their faculties cannot win a full frontal assault on the status issue. The status issue needs to be redefined. Chapter 4 is about research and scholarship. Along with status, it is how research and scholarship are handled that determines how happy the campers are at SCUs. Chapters 5 and 6 are the people chapters, in which I describe faculty life, students, and the community of the SCUs. In Chapter 7, I argue that faculty members at SCUs can have a balanced, interesting academic career while serving students and the larger community.

2 Roots of SCUs: A History of Diversity

Public comprehensive universities are a diverse class of institutions with several histories. A comprehensive history of SCUs has not been written. I provide a brief overview of the limited information available. SCUs have at least seven identifiable sets of roots (Finnegan, 1991), but for the purposes of this overview I focus on five. Finnegan (1991) listed 331 public comprehensives from the 1987 Carnegie classification of which 207 have their roots in teacher academies, normal schools, and/or teachers colleges. The bulk of this chapter traces the history of the normal schools and teachers colleges.

Teacher Training Roots

As late as the 1990s the history of institutions that trained teachers had been largely ignored. As Johnson (1989) wrote, "we know little about what actually went on in these schools" (p. 237). However, Ogren's work (Ogren, 1995, 2003, 2005) has greatly increased what we know about life in normal schools. She has provided a rich description of the academic and social lives of normal school students (the students were called *normalities*) by researching individual institutions' histories, normal school catalogs, student publications, and other archived resources from a broad sampling of normal schools. From Ogren's work it is clear that normal schools provided a form of higher education to what we now call *nontraditional* students, ones who were older, more middle and lower class, and more likely to be female than the students who populated the traditional four-year colleges of the late 19th and 20th centuries. There also are other sources of historical information on normal schools. Many former normal schools have detailed institutional histories, often written by faculty members (see Ogren, 2005 for examples). The development of normal schools is also included in histories of education in individual states (e.g., Jackameit, 1973; Leloudis, 1996). Perhaps what is most striking about these various historical sources is the consistent picture they paint of the early development of normal schools across states and regions.

Many of the distinctive qualities of the present SCUs, positive and negative, are traceable to the nature of the normal schools and their progeny, the teachers colleges. It is unlikely that even a single faculty member at an SCU who originally taught at a teachers college is still teaching, but the traditions of those schools live on in institutional structures and attitudes. There are also many active faculty members at all kinds of institutions who were taught by products of the normal schools and teachers colleges (I for one remember well a teacher in the early 1960s, Mrs. Allworth, who was at least 100 years old and must have been educated at a normal school). The organization of SCUs, the American Association of State Colleges and Universities (AASCU) has its roots in the Association of Teacher Education

Institutions. Among the present day SCUs that were once normal schools and teachers colleges are many of the state-supported universities in Massachusetts, New York, Pennsylvania, California, New Jersey, North Carolina, Michigan, Wisconsin, Texas, Washington, and many other states (see the list provided in the appendix of Ogren, 2005).

Academies and Normal Schools to Teachers Colleges

In the 19th century, public education through what today we would call middle school became increasingly available in most communities. Citizens believed that a basic education was important for their children's cultural, economic, and/or spiritual development. Prominent citizens worked together to create common (elementary) schools in their neighborhoods. An immediate problem was the lack of trained teachers. In many 19th-century common schools, especially in rural areas, the teacher was a young woman, barely older than her students. The shortage of teachers and the concern for teacher qualifications led community leaders, first in New England, to create new institutions for preparing teachers (Altenbaugh & Underwood, 1990; Goodlad, 1990; Herbst, 1989; Ogren, 2005). These new institutions, called *normal schools* after the French term for a teacher training institute, *école normale*, were modeled after European teacher seminaries. The first American normal school was started in Lexington, Massachusetts, in 1839 by Horace Mann (it moved later to Framingham). Mann believed that normal schools were "a new instrumentality in the advancement of the race" (as cited in Wesley, 1957, p. 79). Soon similar institutions were founded in Barre and Bridgewater, Massachusetts. The early normal schools provided prospective teachers with a review of basic knowledge, some elementary ideas about the art of teaching, some background in the government of the school, and experience in a model school. "In some cases the faculty was not much better prepared than the students" (Harcleroad, Sagen, & Molen, 1969, p. 21). The leaders of the early normal schools tended to be ministers or politicians, so the programs were weak on pedagogy and did not see the need to foster students' creativity, imagination, or critical thinking (Altenbaugh & Underwood, 1990). Exceptions were the more pedagogically sophisticated normal schools in Oswego, New York, and Normal, Illinois (Harper, 1935). Many of the normal schools grew out of academies that were essentially high schools. For many years these academies coexisted with teacher preparation programs. How long it took to become certified to teach (degrees were not usually granted by normal schools) depended on how much education and experience the student had before coming to the normal school.

For much of their early history the normal schools prepared mostly women for teaching in elementary grades, a job degree-granting colleges did not want. Herbst (1989) called such preparation "the unfashionable cause." By the last part of the 19th century, many normal schools were branching into the education of secondary school teachers and administrators, tasks that formerly had been left to the private colleges. Most institutions with their roots in the normal schools were not considered collegiate until the 1920s or 1930s when they became state teachers colleges (Harcleroad et al., 1969). The education provided by a normal school tended to be eclectic, with a mixture of the practical and more traditional collegiate subjects such as literature, mathematics, and logic.

The normal schools were not highly thought of in many quarters. One of the most thorough critiques of the normal approach is Holland's 1912 examination of the normal schools in Pennsylvania. Before 1900 the Pennsylvania normal schools had been private corporations owned by stockholders who could hire and fire faculty members and administrators at will. Because profits were at stake, high enrollment was important and every effort was made to ease entrance requirements. Students were often admitted in the middle of a term: "Practically no student, regardless of his age or preparation, has ever been refused [admittance] to any normal school in the state" (Holland, 1912/1972, p. 43). The curriculum designed to meet this diversity of preparation was a hodge-podge of courses from common school, high school, college, and teacher education levels. At one school prospective teachers who came for a three-year program received 3,597 credit hours of education, 2,397 of which were actually in high school subjects.

According to Holland (1912/1972), many of the faculty members at normal schools supplemented their incomes by teaching in institutes for county school systems during afternoons and evenings, even at times that interfered with their duties at the normal school. Recruiters for the normal schools emphasized that students could quickly obtain certification and still experience "the athletic events, the social affairs, the freedom granted to all, and a minimum of distasteful and difficult work" (Holland, p. 57). Holland obtained detailed histories of 265 of the faculty members at

Pennsylvania normal schools. Over half had attended a normal school, often the one they taught at. Of the 265, 117 had only a bachelor's degree, 47 had master's degrees (but only half were earned), and 22 had doctorates (fewer than half earned). Some faculty members had been superintendents or principals, but most of the faculty members had been common school or grade school teachers. Almost half of the faculty members were women (average salary, $782; men made $1,176). Many faculty members had coaching and dormitory duties in addition to six recitations each day with class sizes in the 50–60 range (according to Harcleroad et al., 1969, student-faculty ratios were often 30 to 1 as late as the 1930s). Faculty members had little opportunity for self-improvement. Only a third had done any additional advanced study after first being hired. "Scholarship is not in considerable demand in any one of the institutions" (Holland, p. 78). Holland blamed profit-hungry trustees for the situation. Low pay led to institutional inbreeding and the hiring of weak faculty members from other normal schools.

The profit-making character of the Pennsylvania normal schools probably exacerbated problems that were apparent in many states (Herbst, 1989). Normal schools were under pressure from governmental sources to fill the classrooms of the growing number of public schools with teachers and under pressure from community members to provide a place in which their children could receive advanced education, whether they went on to teach or not. The high school–academy component of the normal schools disappeared early in the 20th century. Normal school faculty members wanted their institutions to change to degree-granting teachers colleges, thus increasing their status. In 1920 there were 46 teachers colleges and 137 normal schools. By 1933 there were 50 normal schools and 146 teachers colleges. Seven years later the term *normal school* could only be found in institutional histories and the front pieces of old library books.

The rapid evolution of two-year normal schools to four-year teachers colleges occurred nationwide. It was not always an easy transition. Becoming teachers colleges meant changing admission standards, curriculum, and faculty qualifications (Pangburn, 1932). The period of training changed from two years to four or five. The curriculum expanded to include more academic work, especially in the traditional liberal studies. Institutions began to offer collegiate degrees and to seek accreditation. Faculty members' teaching loads (often 24 hours of class contact per week or more at the normal schools) decreased to 12–15 hours, and expectations for scholarship increased. Debates about the relative emphasis on the professional (pedagogy) and traditional academic subjects in the curriculum raged on campuses and at professional meetings. The granting of degrees rather than certificates began in the 1910s and 1920s. According to Kent (1930), the Association of American Universities (AAU) commissioned a committee to explore whether students from teachers colleges should be admitted to AAU member graduate schools. The committee reported data on the degrees held by faculty members at the teachers colleges who responded to a questionnaire they distributed. An average of 45 faculty members were at the 71 responding teachers colleges, 2 with doctorates, 13 with master's degrees, 15 with bachelor's degrees, and 15 with no college degree. The AAU decided to admit graduates of teachers colleges on an individual basis with emphasis on checking transcripts for strong course sequences. Learned and Wood (1938) found that in at least one state (Pennsylvania), prospective teachers at four-year institutions were considerably better prepared academically than those at two-year schools (including some of the old normal schools).

Although the focus remained on teacher preparation at the teachers colleges, the apparent continuity of the centrality of teacher preparation throughout the changes hides another continuity. Normal schools and teachers colleges have often been seen as single-purpose institutions, existing to prepare teachers. There is considerable evidence that from very early in the normal school history the normal schools, and later teachers colleges, provided higher education to people who subsequently served in a broad range of vocations (Altenbaugh & Underwood, 1990; Herbst, 1989). Even at the earliest New England normal schools, more than half of the normalities had no intention to teach: "Their motivation was not scholarly learning but basic vocational preparation or improvement" (Herbst, p. 219). Increasingly so into the 20th century, a normal school education was seen as a means for upward social mobility independent of a teaching career. In his 1912 report, Holland criticized the Pennsylvania normal schools for not ensuring that their students were committed to teaching. Because more students meant more profit, courses in stenography, bookkeeping, music, art, and history were added so that the normal schools became institutions "for teaching almost anything" (Holland, 1912/1972, p. 39; see also Elsbree, 1939, on the academic nature of the normal school curriculum).

Many of the teachers colleges carried that name for only 25 years or so, roughly over the period between the world wars. In many ways it would have been difficult to distinguish the teachers colleges from other four-year, undergraduate-oriented institutions. The majority of students would have professed to be interested in a teaching career, but may never have become teachers. No precise figures are available, but as teachers colleges evolved into state colleges, fewer full-time faculty members came directly out of public elementary and high schools, and more obtained a doctorate (or were ABD) before becoming college professors. For the most part the teachers colleges were a transitional form of institution that bridged the normal schools and the state colleges.

Legacies of the Normal School/Teachers College Roots

While we need to be wary of Whig history (interpreting the past through today's eyes), a number of positive and negative qualities of many of the present day SCUs seem to be clear outgrowths of their normal school/teachers college roots. The negative qualities arguably include:

- A tendency to overextend faculty and curricula to serve all people in all ways
- Low standards for admitting and evaluating students and for evaluating faculty members
- A curriculum that is often unfocused and lacks depth
- A strong emphasis on vocationally oriented programs
- Heavy involvement in low-status teacher preparation that brings down the overall status of the institution
- A vulnerability to pressure from state and local governments and accreditation agencies

Positives include:
- A tradition of engagement with the local community, region, and state with positive influences on the local economy, education, and culture
- A general democratic attitude about student access, which allows students to succeed or fail depending on their willingness to avail themselves of the supports provided by the institution, with an emphasis on the development of talent instead of its mere recognition
- A tradition of offering a wide variety of programs that enrich the region
- An emphasis on vocationally oriented programs that are attractive to students who do not want to be doctors, lawyers, or college professors
- Heavy involvement in teacher preparation, which provides a major service to the state and nation, and which can provide a core system of valuing students, teachers, and learning

State Colleges to Regional Comprehensives

The teachers colleges did not last long. Based on the data about name changes provided by Ogren (2005, see Appendix), the median time the former normal schools were teachers colleges before becoming state colleges was only 24 years. Most became state colleges just before World War II or soon after. Some institutions experienced resistance from the existing four-year colleges and universities when they wanted to expand their curricula. Just like the term *normal school* before it, the label *teachers college* disappeared and was largely gone by the early 1960s. During the 1920s and 1930s teachers college administrators knew that many of their graduates would not teach, but for political reasons students were still required to obtain teacher training (legislators wanted to believe they were staffing the schools with well-prepared teachers). Someone who wanted to go into business took accounting and shorthand but with "pedagogy of _____" included where the blank was filled by "accounting" or "shorthand."

After the second world war many of the teachers colleges became state colleges, but they did not grow rapidly immediately. It is not clear why. Perhaps many were not in a fiscal or physical position to handle the influx of veterans. By the late 1950s and early 1960s at least four factors had changed the rate of growth:
• Concerns about educating the baby boomers
• The perceived need for higher qualifications for teachers generated by the Sputnik scare (and the federal dollars that were then provided for prospective teachers)
• The availability of student deferments to avoid the military draft
• A growing expectation (fueled by the federal government starting in the Truman administration) that citizens had a right to higher education

Enrollment in state colleges soared from 299,000 students in 1954 to 1,300,000 in 1966. Most of the state colleges expanded their curricula greatly during the 1950s and 1960s. Added to the traditional education programs (which remained the largest programs at many state colleges for some time) were programs for business and then the helping professions. These programs appeared despite frequent opposition to applied education from arts and sciences faculties (Harcleroad, et al., 1969). As institutions grew, more faculty members were needed in the arts, sciences, social sciences, and humanities to support general education components of the curriculum. Some departments in these areas became large enough to support majors. At many SCUs English, history, and philosophy degrees were offered, not because of the demands of students, administrators, or legislators, but because faculty members fresh from their doctoral programs wanted to teach advanced courses in their disciplines to students who were interested in their disciplines. One outcome of these curricular changes was tension between faculty members who wanted to emphasize basic research and pure knowledge and the teacher educators who had long been in charge but now had low status in the expanding universities (Goodlad, 1990; Labaree, 2004).

By 1969, Harcleroad et al. (1969) saw a growing difference between the state colleges, which had recently been state teachers colleges, and a growing number of regional universities. The major distinction was that the regional universities put more stress on research. Some of the institutions Harcleroad et al. noted were on their way to the doctoral status that they would reach in the 1980s (e.g., College of William and Mary, Ball State University), but most were simply becoming modern comprehensive universities. Harcleroad et al. could foresee that those regional universities provided a model for others to follow. Indeed, the emulation of the research model, at least in campus rhetoric, was beginning to have an effect throughout the tier as more Ph.D.s of prestigious research universities joined the faculties. Harcleroad et al. warned that these new faculty members could take over their universities as "somewhat pale carbon copies" (p. 2) of those they had come from, shutting the door to their students as they worked on their research. Harcleroad et al. called for the regional universities to differentiate themselves (or for their system heads to do so for them) by emphasizing teaching, applied research, service, and the practical over the theoretical.

What happened? Why did the evolution from normal schools to teachers colleges to state colleges and regional universities occur so quickly? Many factors were at play, but three seem especially important. First is the already mentioned pressure from students and communities to broaden the curriculum for those who wanted more education, but did not want to teach and also did not want to leave their region to get more education. The upward social mobility afforded at normal schools and then at teachers colleges and state colleges at a low price helped the leaders of the SCUs form a broader vision.

The second set of pressures for rapid evolution stems from issues of status. The normal schools of the 19th century were secondary schools and therefore low in status relative to degree-granting colleges. In one- to three-year programs most normal schools prepared low-status common (elementary) school teachers while the colleges prepared secondary school teachers and administrators. Being associated with teacher preparation has always conveyed low status (see Herbst, 1989; Johnson, 1989; Labaree, 2004). The first move to change status by the normal schools was a retreat from focusing on the preparation of elementary school teachers: "They wanted to shake their traditional status of precollegiate institutions and to take on the prestige and work of colleges and universities" (Herbst, 1989, p. 232). Altenbaugh and Underwood (1990) put it bluntly: "Pretentious normal school pedagogues wanted the prestige of preparing professionals instead of training lowly elementary teachers" (p. 152). Throughout the first half of the 20th century, college administrators at all levels moved their institutions away from teacher preparation. Elite universities dropped their education programs altogether or limited their involvement to the education of higher-level administrators and researchers, ignoring the preparation of classroom teachers. As we have seen, more and more faculty members wished to increase their status and that of their colleagues by emulating the research model (see Chapter 4). Historically, the emulation probably began much earlier than the 1960s but accelerated through the 1960s and into the 1970s.

The third set of pressures behind the rapid evolution of the SCUs is an expansion of the first. More than just serving as a means of upward social mobility, the history of the SCUs is a history of increasing access for students. Of course, the entire history of American higher education is one of increasing access. However, much of the increase in participation in higher education, even the tremendous changes brought about by the GI Bill, was for a relatively select group. When the state colleges of the 1950s and 1960s expanded their missions in the 1970s and 1980s, they brought in new populations of students that had been excluded (as did the community college movement that followed closely). Students who were less well prepared, academically or culturally, who represented minorities, or who were first-generation college students benefited. Dunham (1969) called the state colleges the "colleges of the forgotten Americans." Herbst (1989) argued that it was the normal schools, not the land-grant universities, that really brought higher education to the people: "With the normal schools, true democracy began in higher education" (p. 231). Some normal school students and teachers college students went into public education. Many did not. Most of the latter would not have had any collegiate experience if it were not for normal schools, teachers colleges, or state colleges. Geiger (2005), in a brief history of higher education that generally ignored the role of the teachers colleges and SCUs, did recognize that "as heirs to the normal schools, they provided access to higher education for a broad segment of the population, especially women" (p. 58).

Nonteacher-Education Roots

Although a majority of present-day SCUs have their roots in the teacher training institutions, there are many with other backgrounds (see Finnegan, 1991). I briefly describe the main categories and give an example or two of each.

Private Roots

Some SCUs started as private two- or four-year colleges, often with a religious, denominational sponsorship. Sometimes the needs of a state for geographical expansion of their college system or pressures from local legislators or other supporters coincided with financial difficulties at a private school. The University of Tennessee–Chattanooga was a private school for 83 years before combining with Chattanooga City College (a two-year school) under the University of Tennessee system umbrella. Boise State began in 1932 as a two-year college sponsored by the Episcopal Church. It became a four-year college 33 years later and grew rapidly. In 1969 it entered the Idaho system of higher education as Boise State College.

Land-Grant, Agricultural-Technical Roots

A number of the current SCUs began as technical schools (often at the secondary level, like the normal schools). Several of the Historically Black Colleges and Universities fit this category. The second Morrill Act in 1890 included a separate-but-equal compromise to desegregation of the existing land-grant colleges that allowed Southern states to develop separate colleges for African Americans. Examples include North Carolina A&T State University and Delaware State University. Like at the normal schools, the level of education provided at these schools was precollegiate. Over time, the historically black schools suffered from the underfunding that typified the separate-but-equal doctrine and were frequently in fiscal straits well into the 20th century. Like the normal schools, the agricultural and technical schools went through phases of being secondary schools, two-year schools, four-year colleges, and, finally, universities. In doing so, they expanded their curricula and widened their appeal to prospective students who otherwise would not have received a postsecondary education. Some institutions that have agricultural roots also have other roots. For example, Georgia Southern University began as a district agricultural school in 1906 but soon became a teachers college, and then followed the typical pattern of becoming a state college and regional university.

Branch Campus Roots

Many of the most recent additions to the SCU category started as extensions of major research universities or other SCUs. The closeness of the ties between the main campus and the branch has varied a good deal from situation to situation. Sometimes the state used existing governing boards and central administrations to avoid starting entirely new institutional organizations. In other cases, campuses started as real extensions of the main campus with faculty members traveling from one site to another or began as two-year feeders that originally focused on general education. In Indiana, Indiana University and Purdue University began branch campuses (separately or together) that became increasingly independent, but never completely so. Similar patterns have occurred in Texas (under the University of Texas and Texas A&M systems), sometimes resulting in very complex histories. For example, Texas A&M–Corpus Christi has had at least four different names since 1970. California State University–Northridge began as a branch campus of the Los Angeles State College of Applied Arts and Sciences (now California State University–Los Angeles) in 1956, then became San Fernando Valley State College two years later. It acquired its current name in 1972.

New Universities

Some SCUs are simply new ventures, although usually with some ties to another institution or its governing board. For example, Saginaw Valley State University started as a private college in 1963 but was taken over by the Michigan system of state-supported colleges just two years later. Community leaders had lobbied in the Michigan legislature for a four-year college for many years before Saginaw Valley was founded. California State University–San Marcos was founded by a legislative act in 1989. It resulted from decades of work by community leaders who felt a university would have a positive impact on the region. A common feature of the new colleges is they have developed in rapidly growing communities in which the local leadership was willing to pressure the state government to support higher education in their areas. Their brief histories are 20th-century versions of what happened in the early development of the normal schools. Members of the community wanted their children to have affordable access to higher education without going too far from home. A four-year university is one requisite facility in a growing community, a sign that the community has matured.

Common Legacies and Present Status

Although histories of SCUs are diverse and the histories of the nonteacher education SCUs are different in detail from that of the former teachers colleges, there are important commonalities. First, regardless of the details of their roots, the SCUs share a common history of strong community support. The SCUs have always been closely tied to the economic, educational, and cultural needs and fortunes of their regions. They indeed are the people's universities. Second, regardless of when they were founded, the SCUs emphasize applied programs. Teacher education is usually part of that applied orientation. Third, SCUs have a history of serving a nonelite student audience. Access, not selectivity, has characterized the histories of the SCUs. Fourth, the history of the SCUs has been a history of emphasizing good teaching. Mission statements of departments and universities at SCUs focus on teacher-student interaction and high quality teaching. Fifth, SCUs have a history of spreading themselves thin, trying to be all things to all people. The spreading includes trying to stretch the curriculum to fit noneducation students, taking programs to geographically remote reaches, offering services to many off-campus groups, and trying to do cutting-edge research. Finally, SCUs, regardless of their histories, share the plight of low status (see Chapter 3). Perhaps the clearest, simplest indication of their low status is their vulnerability to name changes. As new ventures, some of the newest SCUs have avoided the tensions between faculty members with different kinds of backgrounds (master's degrees in education versus doctorates in academic disciplines), but they have not been able to reach the heights of status found at the major research universities or the elite liberal arts colleges.

In those areas of the country that are struggling (particularly the Northeast and parts of the Rust Belt), many SCUs have to deal with stagnant or declining enrollments and state support. In much of the South and in California SCUs are growing rapidly but still suffer from the shift away from state support of higher education. Many SCUs are caught between declining state support accompanied by increasing state control on the raising of tuition and fees. Financial difficulties have been exacerbated by a spate of criticisms of all higher education from outside and from inside (e.g., Anderson, 1992; Douglas, 1992; Hersh & Merrow, 2005; Lewis, 1997; Schaefer, 1990; Smith, 1990; Sperber, 2000; Sykes, 1988). The critics say colleges are too expensive and inefficient. Faculty members spend too much time on their own research and not enough on students and teaching. Faculty members are not accountable. Universities are not sensitive to the needs of their communities. In many ways the SCUs have been less guilty of some of the sins in these common accusations. They have focused on teaching, have kept tuition low, have been responsive to student (and parent) interests in vocationally oriented education, and have been responsive to legislative pressures to aid local and regional economies.

Although most SCUs are relatively healthy, their histories suggest they need to address some major issues. First, SCUs have to deal with the problems of institutional and individual status. Whether the institution's roots are in the normal schools, in failed private schools, or in the malls of mushrooming suburbs, the universities and their faculties need to make peace with their histories and uncouple their self-assessments of status from that of the research universities (see Chapter 3). Second, SCUs need to reduce the curriculum tensions between the pure and applied and the implicit status and values associated with each. Third, SCUs need to find a reasonable balance among the faculty's emphases on teaching, service, and research (see Chapter 4). Finally, SCUs need to find their overall niche in American higher education, one that distinguishes them from research universities and from community colleges (Boyer, 1990).

3 Status and Prestige at SCUs

Status and prestige are driving forces in higher education. Although academics are often stereotyped as raving liberals, they often are fundamentally very conservative, relying on rigid hierarchies of status and prestige (e.g., Aitkin, 1991; Eble, 1962; Mandell, 1977). "Prestige remains the oxygen of higher education" (Burke, 1988, p. 114); universities use prestige to attain resources (Gamson, 1997). The quest for higher status permeates many of the kinds of decisions administrators and governing boards make at all levels. At one time the desire to move up in status was displayed in informal decisions and occasional passing references. In the 1970s the Carnegie Foundation for the Advancement of Teaching (unintentionally, I think), created a classification system that reified the status hierarchy. Research II universities worked to become Research Is, Doctoral I universities worked to become Research IIs, Master's I tried to be Doctoral IIs, and so forth. Dozens of colleges became universities (see Morphew, 2002). Of course, some Liberal Arts I colleges had their own hierarchy that allowed them to opt out of the competition. Public community colleges also were (and are) firm enough in their mission and identity to avoid the status game (public two-year colleges have often attempted to move to four-year status, sometimes because they thought it would help them survive, regardless of status). The general trend has been for newer and lower status institutions to follow the elite in what Riesman (1965) called the "great snake of American academia" (p. xxx).

The quest for institutional status and prestige moved out of the realm of informal lore and into increasing public awareness with the advent of the *U.S. News & World Report (USN&WR)* rankings (Ehrenberg, 2002). Institutions found that they could improve their ratings by manipulating certain *USN&WR* input variables (e.g., increasing entering SAT scores, turning down excellent students who were unlikely to enroll to increase yield, increasing percentage of alumni contributing), which became targets of institutional strategic planning. Because reputation ratings are a large component in determining overall rankings, public relations efforts directed at the potential raters (as well as potential students and their parents) have become common.

Status is also a major factor for individual faculty members. Part of individual status is determined by institutional affiliation. Individual status for faculty members is also closely tied to status within their disciplines. Faculty members are sensitive about their standing relative to their peers. How professionally satisfied faculty members are at an institution can be closely tied to their perception of relative status.

In this chapter I discuss the issues of institutional and individual status at state comprehensive universities. I will start by mapping out the features of the status problem at SCUs and how institutions deal with the status issue in various productive and unproductive ways. Then I will argue that a faculty member's contentment

and relative productivity are tied closely to the willingness to deal in constructive ways with the status issue.

Institutional Status

In Fall 2000 Jeffery Selingo wrote an article for *The
Chronicle of Higher Education*, about the new Nevada
State College in Henderson, Nevada; the title of this
article was replete with status implications: "Facing
new missions and rivals, state colleges seek a makeover:
Can the undistinguished middle child of public higher
education find a fresh identity?" (p. A40). Selingo quoted from Gordon K. Davies, president of the Kentucky
Council on Postsecondary Education, about the need
for the makeover: "If state colleges try to do what they
have always done, they will become a backwater of
American higher education." (p. A40). In his article,
Selingo provided a brief description of SCUs, their
name changes, their expansions beyond teacher education, their faculties' desires not to be associated with
teacher education, and the resulting picture of SCUs as
lesser versions of flagship universities. He pointed out
that many supporters of SCUs see them providing
access to four-year education for local students. He also
noted that critics see the changes at SCUs as "mission
creep" and as a basis for a loss of institutional identity.
Selingo quoted Goodlad about how the SCUs go
through 30-year cycles and now "have to get back to a
reality many of them don't want" (p. A41). Finally,
Selingo reported that in 2000, Nevada leaders were
determined not to lose mission focus: "[SCUs] mish-
mashed their missions, weakened their standards, let
everyone in the door, and suddenly no one wanted to go

there. We can't let that happen here," (p. A42), Mark Alden, a member of the state's Board of Regents said. (Nevada State College opened with a special emphasis on preparing teachers and nurses, the needs of business, and the desires and demands of students.)

Selingo (2000) gave the SCUs attention that the SCUs as a group do not normally receive from the *The Chronicle of Higher Education*. Subsequently, the *Chronicle* published letters by faculty members at Fitchburg State College (Bisk, 2000) and Bridgewater State College (Domingo, 2000), indicating the advantages of SCUs, including small classes, high levels of student-faculty contact, and a general emphasis on teaching. Also published was the letter of R. Barbara Gittenstein, president of The College of New Jersey. President Gittenstein (2000) called Selingo's article an unfair and inaccurate description of the SCUs, claiming that some SCUs were competitive for the best students with schools like the University of Virginia, the University of North Carolina–Chapel Hill, and the College of William and Mary. Norma J. Rees, president of California State University–Hayward (now CSU–East Bay) posted a similar but more defiant response on the university's web site (Rees, 2001). Her claim was that CSU–Hayward was not in the middle, but in the center, fulfilling the comprehensive university mission, not in need of a makeover, but continually changing. President Rees defended CSU–Hayward's role in serving under-served students, offering unique programs, and providing support to California's schools.

Was Selingo (2000) off base about SCUs' "undistinguished middle child" status? Or, indeed, in the range of perceptions of components of American four-year higher education, do the SCUs inhabit a particularly low status neighborhood? That term may be particularly picaresque, but the SCUs and their previous incarnations have long been seen by observers of higher education as undistinguished. Among the descriptions are "weaker universities," "poor-boy schools," "run-of-the-mill universities," "unproductive universities," "universities in a permanent state of academic adolescence," "academic Siberia (or Alaska)," and "institutions that are of 'higher learning' only by the most charitable of definitions" (see Bogue & Aper, 2000; Henderson & Kane, 1991; Lewis, 1997; van den Berghe, 1970). In his classic study of academics, Clark (1987) called the comprehensive category "confusing," saying, "This institutional zone has been a somewhat uncomfortable one for professors; one's academy is neither a true university nor a four-year liberal arts college, but an unsure hybrid often seeking to change its spots" (p. 20). *SCUs have a status problem.* Even when President Gittenstein (2000) attempted to defend the honor of the SCUs, she did so by making reference to higher status schools. What accounts for this low status (standing in the profession) and prestige (reputation based on previous achievement)?

History and the Low Status of SCUs

One source of the low status of many SCUs is their history as normal schools and teachers colleges (see Chapter 2). Teacher education has, over the past century and a half, been subject to a withering barrage of criticism. As Labaree (1997, 2004) has pointed out, those involved in the teaching profession suffer from its association with low status groups. Normal schools and teachers colleges dealt with women—women who were largely from working class backgrounds, women who worked with children, and men and women who wanted to be thinkers and intellectuals, not doers. Labaree (1997) sees the development of the normal schools to teachers colleges to SCUs as a response to market forces. The outcome has not been positive for teachers, teacher educators, or the institutions in which teachers are taught to teach: "Market forces have treated teacher education quite badly over the past 150 years, assigning it to a position of meager prestige and influence and forcing it to adopt practices that have frequently proved educationally counterproductive" (p. 224). Labaree argues that teacher training institutions were forced by market forces and legislative fiat to lower standards in the selection and education of teachers. This had a devastating impact on status. Moreover, many of the students at the normal schools and teachers colleges did not want to be teachers (see Chapter 2); they wanted a quick and easy route to a higher education.

The normal school or teachers college was only one of the roots of SCUs. Have the schools without those undistinguished pedigrees escaped low status? The universities that had been financially troubled private schools did not bring high status to their new public identity. Institutions that had been two-year schools also did not bring high status. Although some had strong histories of service, especially those in rapidly growing urban areas, and were in healthy condition at the time of their transition to four-year universities, they would not have been considered high in status. The historically black universities that had land-grant origins have always suffered from status problems. The newest institutions, while often having substantial local support, have none of the history or tradition that accompanies status. So, one common feature of the various histories of the SCUs is low status in the rigid hierarchy of American higher education. Perhaps the most concrete indication of low status among SCUs is the number of name changes they have experienced. Changing your name is a cry for more attention.

Prestige Generators

A second possible reason why SCUs have had low status is that they have not done what it takes to gain status and prestige. Have the SCUs had the basic features that could allow them, with the right support and leadership, to have attained status and prestige without losing their mission and identity? According to Brewer, Gates, and Goldman (2002), there are three major "prestige generators" available to institutions of higher education. One is student quality, which is essentially equivalent to selectivity. Universities with higher entering test scores over a long period of time acquire prestige. Faculty members tend to support institutional strategies that increase selectivity. Students who already know a lot when they come to college are easier to teach. Ask a group of faculty members the best way to improve the university and they are likely to say, "get better students." External groups such as the *USN&WR* also like this strategy, giving considerable weight to test scores in computing rankings.

A second major prestige generator is research. Brewer et al. (2002) refer in particular to the amount of federal research support obtained by a university. Historically, a vast proportion of the available federal research pot has gone to a small number of research universities. The aura created by the presence of large research accounts is powerful. For example, one elite research university was listed as having one of the top 25 psychology departments in the nation in a reputation ranking despite the fact that the university has no psychology department. The raters clearly transferred the overall status of the university to all its programs, even programs it might not have. Clark (1987) considered research *the* driving force: "The prestige hierarchy dictates that the research imperative propel the system . . . Individual professors and their institutions ascend in the hierarchy to any substantial degree by investing in research and offering some new results" (p. 101).

The third prestige generator is sports. High visibility in the national press brings name recognition or enhances what is there. Some administrators believe that investments in sports (particularly football and men's basketball) bring attention quickly. At the highest levels of intercollegiate sports, administrators rarely challenge the importance of big-time sports unless a player or coach does something unusually egregious.

How do the SCUs fare in regard to the three major prestige generators? Selectivity is a possible route to prestige for SCUs. However, for SCUs to take the selectivity route to prestige would mean abandoning a fundamental feature in the traditional SCU mission. The core concept of the people's university is the democratization of higher education. The SCU and its preceding institutional types have always strongly emphasized access. SCUs in economically and demographically growing regions have grown bigger rather than becoming more selective. Many SCUs have developed strong honors programs to attract more students with high test scores and grades, but they usually do so while maintaining access for less elite students. SCUs in regions with declining economies or demographics would risk ruin or stagnancy by increasing selectivity, even if they were willing to change their philosophies of accessibility.

The research route to prestige also presents problems for SCUs. As indicated earlier, federal research dollars go to a small number of large research universities. No SCUs appear on the lists of recipients of major research funds. SCUs may have access to funds for training students in underserved disciplines (e.g., some of the sciences, special education) but are much less likely to attract funds for pure research. Training funds do not generate prestige the way research funds do. In many areas (especially science and technology) the initial investment SCUs would have to make to get into the pure research game would be prohibitive. Some larger, richer SCUs on the make (i.e., heading toward Doctorate status in Carnegie terms) may be able to build certain research niches, perhaps related to geographic advantage, but niche-building will generate status in limited ways.

The third prestige generator, involvement in big-time sports, has been used by some universities to their advantage. However, this strategy is expensive and success requires a good deal of luck. Scheduling and conference membership opportunities have to be available. Moreover, sports success, like the competition for federal research dollars, is a zero-sum game in which new winners must take the place of old winners. Faculty members, unlike boosters, may not be supportive of using discretionary funds or student fees to improve sports teams. The wrong coach, long losing streaks or humiliating losses, or a series of incidents of student misbehavior may lead to counterproductive publicity.

In short, SCUs are at a significant disadvantage regarding institutional status (Pattenaude & Bassis, 1990). What can they do?

Building Reputation Rather Than Prestige

Prestige based on the traditional status generators seems to be out of reach for most SCUs. Yet surely there are ways for SCUs to get better and be recognized for that improvement. Brewer et al. (2002) differentiate prestige and reputation. They see both as assets that allow universities to convey nonmonetary information to potential customers. Prestige is an indicator that an institution has done a good job over a long period of time. Reputation is more fluid and more closely related to customer satisfaction. Whereas there are only three major status generators, there are many ways to improve reputation. Brewer et al. note that an institution that is trying to play the prestige game may do so at the risk of its reputation. Wholesale changes in entering test score standards might lead to a loss of identity in the region, but enhancing the honors program could suggest that the institution is trying to do better by strong students. Instituting strong publish-or-perish requirements could cause tension on campus and feed external perceptions of pretentiousness, but supporting faculty research could improve the scholarly climate on campus. Reputations can be enhanced in almost any area at almost any institution. The prestige and status game requires that a positive change in the ranking of one institution is accompanied by a loss of rank by another. All institutions can increase reputation without a loss of reputation by another institution.

Institutional Status—Conclusion

Clara Lovett, former president of the American Association for Higher Education, has pointed out that many of the flagship and other universities are playing the prestige game (Lovett, 2005). The fastest way for them to increase their rankings is by improving their indexes of selectivity (increasing applicant pools without increasing acceptance rates). She argues that this has created a paradox. At a time when there is greater need to provide access to higher education for students from lower-income families, public universities are increasing selectivity, and increasing tuition and fees. Meanwhile, Lovett says, the emphasis on prestige and rankings (status) devalues the hundreds of institutions Dunham (1969) called "colleges of the forgotten Americans." These institutions are the SCUs and the community colleges. Because their more selective peers and the media devalue the less prestigious schools, many students, parents, and school counselors devalue them. Lovett points out that it is these less status-oriented institutions that are more ready to adapt to the changes sought by the employers and legislators outside the academic establishment. Lovett calls these schools "the unsung heroes of higher education" (p. B20) and she argues they deserve more recognition for what they do.

Lovett is right, but it is not really surprising that all kinds of institutions have emulated the research model with its emphases on selective admissions and faculty research. It has the status and there has been no well-delineated alternative of what a university should be (Henderson & Kane, 1991). The SCUs cannot compete in the status game without being pretentious. Boyer (1990) wrote, "It's time to end the suffocating practice in which colleges and universities measure themselves far too frequently by external status rather than by values determined by their own distinctive mission" (p. xiii). There are hints of alternatives to the research model in publications of organizations like AASCU and in examples of institutions that have resisted the drift toward expansive missions (see Morphew, Toma, & Hedstrom, 2001). Models are needed that allow multiple standards of excellence in which institutions can emphasize what they do well rather than emulate the elite research universities, an argument that has been made periodically since the 1960s (Dunham, 1969; Grubb & Lazerson, 2005; Henderson & Kane, 1991). As Grubb and Lazerson more recently put it:

> This would allow regional institutions and second-tier universities to focus on what they do well instead of trying to emulate the elite, to examine how best to serve their regions, to expand conceptions of applied research and useful knowledge, to see how best they could prepare the middle-level students they have rather than the students they would like to have, to develop faculty who are enthusiastic about their teaching roles and public service . . . rather than feeling like wannabe researchers. (pp. 19–20)

Thus, a model for institutional reputation could focus on the SCUs' existing and potential strengths. First, the model could include a major focus on good teaching and student learning. The research model has left this arena wide open. SCUs could continue to find ways to show how students are really changing during their time in college. Second, taking the focus on teaching and learning a step farther, SCUs could be the institutions in which the scholarship of teaching and learning is taken seriously (see Chapter 4 where I review research that shows that SCU faculty members have historically been better represented in pedagogical research than in basic research). SCU faculty could emphasize research of all kinds on the teaching-learning process. "Building a true community of learning in the classroom and finding ways to educate diverse students and evaluate the results is a challenge that seems especially appropriate for the comprehensive college or university" (Boyer, 1990, p. 64). Third, SCUs can expand another historical strength in emphasizing regional engagement through continuing education, applied research, and consultation. Finally, the SCU model might emphasize innovation. Freed from the prestige race, SCUs can afford to take risks in innovative teaching, innovative forms of community engagement, and innovative research that is not constrained by existing paradigms. In short, a weakness, the inability to play the status game, could become a strength.

Individual Status

One source of the ubiquity and power of the research model is the monopoly research universities have in the preparation of faculty members throughout higher education. Faculty members at SCUs are socialized into the research model in their graduate training where expectations are created for low teaching loads, easily attained release time for research, and ample fiscal and physical resource availability. Moreover, new faculty members at SCUs bring with them the values and standards of their disciplines. Productive (i.e., good) faculty members are cosmopolitans, not locals. They spend significant amounts of time away from their campuses and are heavily involved in disciplinary activities such as organizing meetings, obtaining grants, and reviewing and editing journals. They spend less time teaching, serving on committees, or working with local organizations. High status accrues to those who are loyal to their disciplines, not to those who are loyal to their home institutions.

Even when new faculty members at SCUs recognize their environment has changed, their basic sense of what good institutions (or departments) and good faculty members are is governed by research university and discipline values. Finnegan's (1993a; 1993b) research on comprehensive university faculty cohorts suggests that many faculty members who came to SCUs prior to 1972 had been first-generation college students themselves. They chose to work at SCUs because they wanted to emphasize teaching and because they wanted to work with a less elite student population. After the faculty labor market bust in the early 1970s, the SCUs found they could hire graduates of more prestigious research university doctoral programs who were more likely to bring with them the research university value of research first. Some of those faculty members were able to reproduce something like the research university they knew as *the* way a university is supposed to work. However, most have struggled to maintain a sense of identity, self-esteem, and comfort within a new type of institutional experience.

Self-Esteem and Status

William James, the psychologist and philosopher, clearly outlined how individuals acquire a particular level of self-esteem (James, 1890). Self-esteem is a function of successes relative to pretensions. When pretensions are great, successes also must be great or self-esteem will decrease. The problem faced by the SCU faculty member who is using the pretensions of the research university model is that maintaining high successes (publications in prestigious journals, grants from major sources, invitations to speak at international conferences) is difficult under conditions of high teaching loads and meager fiscal and physical resources. If you maintain the same pretensions and fail to succeed at expected levels, your self-esteem is bound to decline.

One of the most vivid published accounts of successes failing to meet pretensions at an SCU is in the writings of Terry Caesar (1991, 2000). For 30 years, Caesar was an English professor at Clarion University in Pennsylvania. Caesar's original appointment occurred when he had not yet completed his doctorate (which was completed after he had been tenured) and Clarion was in transition from Clarion State College to Clarion University. In 1991 his "Teaching at a Second-Rate University" appeared in the *South Atlantic Quarterly*. This article is full of bitter prose about his experience as a scholar who wants to be recognized within his discipline and by his discipline's stars, but who instead is invisible, at least in part, because of his institutional affiliation. A few quotes from the article should provide the flavor:

- "The first thing to say about teaching at a second-rate university, however, may be the last thing: it actually has no reputation at all" (p. 450).

- "Second-rate universities, by definition, aren't news-worthy" (p. 459).
- "Ultimately teaching at a second-rate university is to acknowledge a ceaseless condition of structural exclusion from any decision about what can and cannot be authoritatively said" (p. 462).
- "Teaching at a second-rate university is knowing, at least, that you're not worth knowing" (p. 466).

Also in the article, Caesar made references to Clarion's "woefully provincial student body" (p. 452) and "irremediably mediocre faculty" (p. 452). Caesar remained at Clarion after the article was published. He was interviewed about the article by a reporter for the *The Chronicle of Higher Education*. In a later book (Caesar, 2000), Caesar described the aftermath of his article. Some of his provincial students and mediocre colleagues had hurt feelings. Letters came in from like-minded colleagues at other institutions who also felt invisible. No job offers came from elite universities.

Caesar's experiences and writings reveal a number of ironies. He laments the mediocrity of his colleagues' scholarship while confusing the Carnegie Foundation for the Advancement of Teaching institutional classification system with a nonexistent rating system from the American Association of University Professors. In a chapter in which he derides the writing ability of Clarion students he misspells many words (perhaps he is guilty only of poor proofreading). He shows no awareness of the history of the university he worked at for 30 years. More important, writing about power in the deconstructivist tradition, he fails to fully deconstruct his own assumptions, particularly those about teaching and scholarship. He thinks his article rankled many because some faculty members are not happy "teaching at places where they're supposed to do nothing else" (Caesar, 2000, p. 30). He goes on to ask, "What *is* it to be content to teach? Not to read anything, not to go to conferences, not to have professional ambitions?" (p. 32).

However, perhaps the greatest irony about Caesar is that he had had considerable success in his discipline. He published, went to major conferences, took part in workshops, and served on review panels. It was not enough. Pretensions to fame outweighed the successes. In discussing a response to the *South Atlantic Quarterly* article from a faculty member at another institution, Caesar said: "People react differently to pretense. How an academic reacts may very well determine what sort of career he or she is likely to have" (Caesar, 2000, p. 29). He was exactly right.

Donald Hall, another English professor at an SCU (California State University–Northridge), provides an account in which the facts are quite similar to Caesar's. But Hall views his circumstance in a strikingly different way (Hall, 2002). Like Caesar, Hall takes a deconstructivist approach to "text." For Hall, the target texts are the university as an institution and the self. He asks his readers to question the traditional assumptions of the entrenched academic hierarchy and examine the nature of academic lives outside the research university: "Clearly our profession must do a better job at welcoming voices and perspectives from across its diverse landscape in order to better train new academics and more fully appreciate the varieties of work performed" (p. 23). Instead of falling into cynicism, Hall says, "We must speak out about the pressures and potentials inherent in such work, and at the same time, acknowledge our own responsibility for constructing a career that satisfies us" (p. 23). Hall calls faculty members at "teaching institutions" to redefine success without reference to the research model standards by setting reasonable and productive goals within the mission of a different kind of university.

The Matthew and Podunk Effects

The power of status in academe is nicely captured in two descriptive principles used by sociologists of science. The Matthew Effect, usually attributed to Merton (1968) who took it from the Gospel of Matthew, says that those who have status, resources, and recognition will get more. The Matthew Effect works through a variety of mechanisms. For example, editors frequently invite well-known scholars to write articles and chapters for their journals and books. Grants go to scholars who have track records and facilities. The Matthew Effect results in a growing gap between the haves and have-nots.

The Podunk Effect (Gaston, 1978) says that deserving achievements get less recognition than they should when the achiever is associated with a low-prestige institution. If the Matthew Effect is the result of a halo effect, the Podunk Effect is a result of guilt by association. Terry Caesar's plaints suggest he feels he is a victim of the Podunk Effect. We will never know which budding scholars at SCUs might have accomplished more research and scholarship if the Podunk Effect had not been at work. Indeed, the circularity of the Matthew and Podunk Effects limits their explanatory usefulness, and the data relevant to the Podunk Effect have not given it strong support (Gaston). Yet these effects are descriptive of something that truly does happen and faculty members at SCUs get the short end in each case.

Related to the Matthew and Podunk Effects, and perhaps more interesting for SCUs, is the question of what happens when faculty members, especially new faculty members, attempt to publish or otherwise get recognition for their creative activities. Gaston (1978) summarized the early research on reinforcement for scientific productivity. Basic forms of reinforcement are acceptance of submitted papers and success in grant requests. At a research university, beginning scholars who experience rejection have support systems that make persistence the likely response to failure. Support comes from peers who are interested in their work, from institutional systems that help revise grant applications, and from pressure to be productive. At SCUs scholars who have experienced rejection may not have similar supports to help them persist. They are easily discouraged and never acquire the critical mass of confidence-building experiences that could lead to further work.

Is the Podunk Effect a description of a self-fulfilling process? Do faculty members at SCUs enter a game they can't win? Labaree (2004), in his analysis of the status problems of schools of education, questions the basic assumptions behind the power of the research university model: "There is an element of the confidence game in the market-based pattern of academic life" (p. 202). The confidence game relies on several assumptions that are probably not true. One is that faculty members at prestigious universities know more and can do more. A second assumption is that prestigious faculties make for good universities. Third is that prestigious research makes for good faculty. Of course, a wise scholar of higher education would likely say what makes good faculties and universities depends. It depends on mission. But a Terry Caesar will say that regardless of mission, status, institutional or individual, is all that matters in a world where the *status* hierarchy is so clear. Most SCU faculty members buy right into the assumptions.

What Can SCU Faculty Members Do About Status and Self-Esteem?

Status hierarchies indeed are ubiquitous in higher education. Clark (1987) wrote: "Such hierarchies are an affront to democratic instincts. They produce large numbers of have-nots...to hundreds of thousands of professors developing a sense of relative deprivation as they judge their own successes against that of others who are simply positioned by the system to be better off" (p. 60). Yet Clark is not lamenting the existence of the hierarchy. For him and his ilk, as long as there are opportunities for upward mobility, talent will rise to the top. Every faculty member (and every institution) will work harder.

Anyone who has spent time at SCUs has known some Terry Caesars, although their plaints rarely are so bitter or eloquent. Most of us have some experience with the Podunk Effect, especially those in states where there is a flagship university or two. What can SCU faculty members do about status? How can they avoid low self-esteem? James' (1890) self-esteem equation suggests some possibilities. One route to high self-esteem is to have high success. A faculty member can do those things that have traditionally been seen as successful, including publishing in prestigious journals and obtaining grants. The latter can be used to obtain release time and continue the productivity cycle. Most SCUs have faculty members who follow this route to status and self-esteem, although the numbers who do so are very small (see Chapter 4). There may be functional limits on the number of faculty members who can follow this route without creating problems for units in fulfilling their teaching and service missions (Massy & Zemsky, 1994).

A second strategy for maintaining self-esteem and status is to decrease pretensions. Effective institutional leaders are not likely to encourage this approach. Faculty members with low pretensions are likely to risk obsolescence, stagnation, and low morale. Low but not absent pretensions offer the advantage of reaping results from low levels of success while minimizing failure. Because it is difficult to succeed in the traditional realms of research and publication, keeping pretensions low would seem to be a smart strategy. It is also likely to make institutions and individuals pretty uninteresting.

A third strategy is to redefine pretensions and successes. Just as institutions can opt out of the status game by focusing on reputation, individuals can look at a broader range of faculty activities as appropriate. What "counts" as faculty productivity needs to change. In their reconsideration of the concept of scholarship, Boyer and his colleagues provide a different way to think about pretensions and successes. Boyer (1990) argued that there are multiple forms of scholarship, ones that focus on traditional research, integration of disciplinary concepts, teaching, and applications (see Chapter 4 for details). When Boyer's work on scholarship was first published in 1990, he and others (Leatherman, 1990) saw the potential of the expanded view of scholarship for SCUs. They recognized the special problem of status faced by SCUs. The redefinition of pretensions provides the best hope for SCUs and their faculty members to deal with the status issue. Redefining those pretensions and successes will require a carving out of identities and missions distinct from those of the research universities. It will require new ways to recruit and orient faculty members, new ways to evaluate faculty efforts, and new reward structures consistent with those identities and missions (Henderson & Kane, 1991; Pattenaude & Bassis, 1990). The result could be a more contented and productive faculty. Donald Hall (2002) said redefinition at the "teaching institutions" can work:

> The happiest and most vibrant of us have learned well how to read the texts of our institution, our professions, our careers, and our own professorial self-identities, in open dialogue with each other, so that we have "succeeded" in multi-dimensional ways, even when the larger profession has looked at our institutional affiliation (which is far from prestigious) and implicitly or explicitly defined us otherwise. (p. xxi)

4 Creating Little Harvards: Research and Scholarship at SCUs

Eisenmann (1990) interviewed a West Chester University professor whose career had spanned the period in which his school had changed from a state teachers college to a state college and then a university. From the professor's perspective, the shifts in mission represented by the name changes had been accompanied by a desire on the part of the institution's administration to "create a little Harvard" (Eisenmann, p. 304). The professor's concern was that there had been increasing pressure to publish research findings. Barzun (1991) called this "scholarship at gunpoint." Indeed, scholarship has frequently been equated with publication (sometimes even in disciplines such as theatre, art, and music in which creative products and performances are clearly more important). "Across different types of universities there is but one accepted, valued, and rewarded scholarly goal: to conduct original research and publish it in scholarly, refereed journals" (Lynton, 1983, p. 21). Should the West Chester professor have been concerned? Have SCUs attempted to emulate research universities? How much do faculty members actually publish? Are there forms of scholarship other than published research findings that are worthwhile and worth counting during tenure, promotion, and merit pay processes?

Emulation of the Research Model

Research is considered a major status generator (see Chapter 3). Although an emphasis on research and publication in colleges and universities has a long history, it was only after World War II that emphasis on the idea of "publish or perish" really accelerated (Burke, 1988; Cuban, 1999). One of the major criticisms of higher education has been that the professors have abandoned students for the laboratory or library. Harcleroad, Sagen, and Molen (1969) worried that the trend had spread to SCUs. Blackburn and Lawrence (1995) reported that it had: "The new hires at the regional universities were recruited for their research potential, with the clear message that research will be rewarded" (p. 275). Goodlad (1990) described the process in his discussion of education faculty: "The word was out (usually attributed to a newly appointed provost or academic vice president rumored to be supported by the president): all future promotion decisions will be heavily dependent on research productivity" (p. 24). Further, according to Goodlad, this trend has been especially devastating at "many of the regional public and private universities that only recently had been teachers colleges or dominantly teaching institutions" (p. 24). From 1969 to 1989 the percent of respondents to a Carnegie Foundation for the Advancement of Teaching survey who strongly agreed with the item "in my department it is difficult for a person to achieve tenure if he or she does not publish" increased from 6% to 43% at comprehensive universities. Dey, Milem, and Berger (1997) found that faculty reported increases in publication productivity from the 1970s to the 1990s at all types of colleges and universities, but that the largest increases were reported by faculty members at comprehensive universities. In his advice to the beginning professor, Glover (2001) is blunt about the issue: It is still publish or perish. It is publications that get you hired, publications that get you tenured and promoted, and publications that let you move to a better institution. Glover tells new faculty members to go for quantity early and quality later when they are tenured and settled.

What led to the drift toward the research model? At the research universities, the post–World War II influx of federal support was a major factor (Sperber, 2000). In the 1950s and 1960s large amounts of federal grant funding for basic research flowed to many disciplines, especially in the sciences and social sciences. These funds provided for new facilities, supported graduate students, provided indirect costs to institutions, and generally raised expectations for income beyond tuition, fees, and state support. A second factor in the drift toward research has been the growing strength of the disciplines (Becher, 1989). Status accrues to faculty members who are thought highly of in their disciplines (Bowen & Schuster, 1986; Smith, 1990). Cosmopolitan faculty members are those who are known outside their campuses, who fly off to international conferences, give invited addresses, consult, and engage in other activities testifying that they take an important role within their disciplines. Locals, in contrast, carry the teaching and service loads at their own campuses. Cosmopolitans are paid more and are promoted more often.

Arguably the most important factor in the drift toward research is the monopoly the research universities have on the preparation of faculty members for all kinds of institutions. Graduate schools socialize prospective faculty members into a culture that values research and educates students in the skills to carry out research. For many, if not most, faculty members these values and skills become part of a professional identity. Even faculty members who are not doing research think they should be (Ruscio, 1987). Clark (1987) described the role of research: "The minority of academics who are actively engaged in research lead the profession in all important respects. Their work mystifies the profession, generates its modern myths, and throws up its heroes" (p. 102).

There are numerous constraints on faculty members at SCUs who want to do serious research. Teaching loads at SCUs are typically in the 9–15 semester hour range compared to the 3–6 hour loads more common in research universities. Students at SCUs need and expect more interaction with faculty members. SCUs rarely have the sophisticated facilities or funds for startup costs that many scientists need. Among unionized faculties (which are much more common at SCUs) there may be little incentive to conduct research. Faculty cultures at some SCUs are not research friendly. Research is simply an add-on to traditional expectations for teaching and service. In short, while SCU faculty members may have carried a research value system from their graduate education, actually conducting research requires a high degree of self-motivation and ingenuity in getting around the considerable barriers.

Criticisms of the Research Emphasis

Would it really matter if faculty members, even those at research-oriented universities, did not have the time and resources to do research? The debate about the relative emphasis on teaching and research in the life of faculty members across institutional types is an old one. Critics of a publish-or-perish mentality argue that student learning should be the core activity, while defenders of the research emphasis argue that without research there would be nothing to teach (Light, 1974). The double- (or triple-) threat professor who can do it all well is not a myth, but a rarity, especially outside the elite universities (Fulton & Trow, 1974). Astin and Chang (1995) found a strong negative correlation between a college or university's emphasis on research and its emphasis on teaching and student development. It was rare in their sample of approximately 200 institutions for institutions with a strong research reputation to be even a little above average in student orientation. By using rather liberal definitions of "high" research and "high" student orientation, Astin and Chang did identify 11 institutions with strong student orientations that were above average in research orientation. Almost all the identified colleges (and they were all colleges) were small, highly selective liberal arts colleges. On the other hand, six of the nine institutions that were very low on research- and student-orientations were public four-year colleges that Astin and Chang identified as "mostly former teachers colleges" (p. 47).

In a report on policies concerning faculty members by a coalition of higher education associations (American Association of State Colleges and Universities, 1999), the authors point out that surveys show that research is overvalued (administrators thought by faculty, faculty thought by administrators). Moreover, much of the public still believes "that research is overemphasized with the result that the quality of instruction is diminished" (p. 24). Douglas (1992) argued that faculty members at colleges and universities once viewed undergraduate education as the core mission. Now they are too busy doing society's work through specialization and disciplinary research to care about undergraduate education. Schaefer (1990) argued that too much time is spent on "what more often than not is worthless publication [that] detracts from the time that could and should . . . be spent in preparing classes and working with students" (p. 107). He echoed James' (1903) concern that early specialization can kill creativity. Smith (1990) called it "killing the spirit." In addition to concerns about deemphasizing teaching and the narrowing of the faculty member, Goodlad (1990) and others (Barzun, 1991; Smith, 1990) have pointed out the problem of the inflation (in quantity and quality) of the published literature that would occur if everyone published as much as the rhetoric suggests they should: "If all the professors published at even the level expected or rumored to be expected, there would be a need for thousands of journals in addition to the thousands already serving the academic community" (Goodlad pp. 24–25). Smith (1990) called much of the research that goes on "busywork on a vast, almost incomprehensible scale" (p. 7).

Cochran (1992) questions the assumption that being involved in disciplinary research necessarily indicates anything at all about a faculty member's competence.

What is the functional relationship between teaching and research? There have been some heroic attempts to show that involvement in research is essential to being a good teacher (e.g., Braxton, 1996; Jenkins, Breen, Lindsay, & Brew, 2003). However, a strong position that a good teacher *must* be a good researcher is untenable. As Park (1996) argued, there is a plausible connection between good teaching and ongoing faculty development in the form of attendance at workshops, staying current with research in one's field, and other scholarly activities. A connection between good teaching and publishing makes much less sense. However, it is also true that there is no strong evidence that good teachers are usually unproductive in research. Teaching effectiveness and research productivity appear to be independent (see Feldman, 1987) with two important caveats, both of which have been highlighted by Fairweather (1996, 2002). First is the simple fact that research and teaching each take time. Although there is some evidence that some particularly productive teacher-researchers just work longer hours (Stack, 2003), there is always competition for time (large research grants can help but almost always include "release" from some teaching). Fairweather concludes that the "complete faculty member" is rare. A second caveat is that research productivity is clearly more financially rewarding than good teaching. There is no academic labor market for good teachers. Throughout academe, high salaries are associated with high research productivity.

The criticisms about the overemphasis of research assume that faculty members are spending a great deal of time in research and publishing activities. The next section focuses on the degree to which faculty members in general and faculty members at SCUs in particular spend their time on research and publication activities.

How Much Research Do SCU Faculty Members Do?

Scholars of higher education have argued that the trend toward a publish-or-perish attitude for faculty members from the colleges and universities outside the major research sector is a recent phenomenon, certainly post-1960 (Tang & Chamberlain, 1997). However, the call for higher levels of research productivity at teachers colleges dates to 1931. Sangren (1931a; 1931b), a prominent teachers college administrator (later president of Western Michigan University for 24 years), counted the relative number of research articles, books, and memberships in learned societies across different types of institutions. Sangren's premise was that such numbers were indicative of the quality of an institution's faculty. He found faculty members at the teachers colleges wanting on all counts. "Such facts as these only give additional evidence that the teachers college has not yet been able to take itself off the level of a normal-training school" (Sangren, 1931a, p. 89). Sangren pled for a more scholarly attitude. Teachers college faculty members "should be overflowing with some of the old-time scholastic spirit and enthusiasm which make them spend much more time in the consideration of problems of scholarship and much less time in general college gossip" (1931a, p. 91). He suggested a reduction in teaching loads from 16 to 12 hours would help. Later, Evenden (1938) provided relevant self-report data from a survey of 6,227 teachers college faculty about their research activities over a 5-year period. Across disciplines, 14% had published a book or dissertation and 11% had published 5 or more articles in "well-known periodicals" over the period.

How much old-time scholastic spirit has caught on at the modern SCU? Before directly addressing that question, we need to look at the degree to which publish-or-perish holds across all types of institutions. I begin with the rhetoric, then move to a consideration of the data. Douglas (1992) argues that even at the research universities, many faculty members publish a book or a few articles, get tenured, and then glide. Somehow they still manage to convince administrators, trustees, legislators, and the general public that they are productive. "Doing so is something of a high art, perhaps even bordering on magic" (Douglas, p. 92). Less cynically, perhaps, Becher (1989) points out that publication practices vary according to discipline. Scientists publish more than those in the humanities. Historians are more likely to publish books than are physicists. Within science, chemists publish many small papers, maybe 10–12 per year, and with many coauthors, whereas biologists are more likely to publish only one or two articles per year (unless they are taxonomists who may publish 10–15 short papers per year). Citations to each other's works, a common measure of the impact of research, also differ by discipline. Mathematicians cite few others because they do not want their ideas to be unduly influenced by others. Biologists have to show they have read all the relevant background, and historians have to show they have considered all the arguments. Becher concludes that the softer the area, the more citations are needed.

Perhaps the strongest words on the status of the publish-or-perish question come from a book originally issued in the 1970s but reissued in 1998 with the argument that little had changed. Lewis (1975/1998) reviewed papers by sociologists of science showing that individual publication rates are very low, even in elite universities. Lewis's conclusion is that except for faculty members in the elite of the elites, "the threat to publish or perish is empty . . . academic men [sic] publish or not publish, and few will perish" (p. 40). The myth drives some to publish, but not many and not much, "Thus the publish-or-perish dogma is largely a fraud, perpetuated by the notoriety of a few cases" (p. 41).

Now, to the data. How much are faculty members really publishing? It turns out that is a difficult question to answer. The self-reports of publishing activity provided by the U.S. Department of Education indicate a fairly high rate of nearly two refereed publications per year for full-time faculty members, with the distribution skewed by high rates at research and doctorate universities (U.S. Department of Education, National Center for Education Statistics, 2003). Harder data are provided in a recent report by Toutkoushian, Porter, Danielson, and Hollis (2003). They attacked the problem by using Thomson's 1996 editions of the *Science Citation Index*, the *Social Sciences Citation Index*, and the *Arts and Humanities Citation Index*. Together the three indexes cover more than 6,600 scholarly journals in more than 200 academic disciplines. Using the addresses of approximately 1,300 four-year colleges and universities included in the 1998 edition of *U.S. News & World Report's* "Best Colleges," Toutkoushian et al. counted the number of journal articles from each institution and divided that count by the number of faculty members at each institution. The authors recognized that their procedure underrepresented disciplines that stress books rather than articles.

For the 1,309 institutions Toutkoushian et al. (2003) examined, the number of publications ranged from 0–7,243. The mean number of publications per institution was 168, but that measure of central tendency is misleading because a few institutions have many publications and many institutions have few publications. The median or middle number of publications *per institution* was six publications. Almost 20% of the institutions had no publications in 1996 while 13% had 200 or more. Taking into consideration the number of faculty members per institution, the mean number of publications (listed in the indexes) per faculty member was .26. The rate ranged from 0–7.63 with a median of .056. Using the latter figure, the average institution needed almost 20 faculty members to produce one publication in one of the 6,600 journals covered in 1996. So, across four-year American institutions, it does not appear that publish-or-perish has been taken very seriously. Even if Toutkoushian et al.'s medians are off by a factor of five (highly unlikely because the major forms of publication missing are books and chapters, which are even less common than journal articles) the "average" faculty member is producing a publication every four years. Other available self-report data show that the average faculty member publishes less than 10 items in an entire career, most much less (Fox, 1985).

What about the faculty members at SCUs? Toutkoushian et al. (2003) disaggregated their data by Carnegie classification, but they did not separate public and private institutions, so they only provide data on all comprehensive universities. The mean number of publications for the 398 Master's I institutions was 30

(0.10 per faculty member) and for the 88 Master's II institutions, 4 (0.04). For comparison, the corresponding figures for 83 Research I and 36 Research II universities were 1,886 (2.04) and 548 (0.91), respectively. Publication rates for comprehensive university faculty were lower than those of faculty members from Liberal Arts I schools (0.14). Another way to look at these data is that it took 20 comprehensive university faculty to produce as many publications as one Research University I faculty member did in 1996. No matter how the data are parsed, faculty members at comprehensive universities are publishing at modest rates in either absolute or relative terms. Moreover, because most journal articles are cited by others only once or never (Braxton & Bayer, 1986; Creamer, 1998), the work being done at comprehensive universities has little impact.

Toutkoushian et al.'s (2003) data combine private and public comprehensive universities. Perhaps the private comprehensives bring down the overall average. To check, Heidi Buchanan and I (Henderson & Buchanan, 2006a) searched the same database (covering more than 6,600 journals in more than 200 disciplines) used by Toutkoushian et al. for 50 randomly chosen SCUs. We looked at the number of publications for each of the 50 institutions by decade for the 1960s, 1970s, 1980s, and 1990s. The number of publications ranged from 0–1,563 per institution across the decades. For the four decades the average number of publications per institution was 16.9 for the 1960s, 180.0 for the 1970s, 303.4 for the 1980s, and 381.4 for the 1990s. Because institutions had tripled in size on average, we adjusted for the number of faculty members by using the number of faculty members at the institution in the middle of each decade. The resulting mean rates of publication per faculty member were .08 for the 1960s, .39 for the 1970s, .63 for the 1980s, and .65 for the 1990s. These means were significantly different from each other except for the final two. Overall it is clear that rate of publishing has been increasing until recently, but the rate of publishing is quite low. To provide some perspective on the rates from SCUs, the comparable figures for the decades for Harvard University were .24, 11.33, 23.93, and 32.16. For the University of North Carolina University–Chapel Hill they were .69, 6.56, 12.94, and 14.50. And for Swarthmore College, they were .62, 3.51, 5.94, and 6.02.

Because both Toutkoushian et al.'s (2003) and our data are for institutions rather than individuals, it is impossible to know whether a few individuals account for the bulk of publications. However, we know from other research (e.g., Alpert, 1985; Price, 1986) that a minority of faculty members in scientific fields produce most of the publications and even more of the publications that have a major impact. "Scientists have a strong urge to write papers but only a relatively mild one to read them" (Price, 1986, p. 62). Regardless of what is going on at the individual level, it is clear for the SCUs, publish-or-perish is an overstatement. The conflict between comprehensive university faculty member perceptions of emphasis on publishing and the reality of publishing was apparent in the 1989 national survey sponsored by the Carnegie Foundation (Boyer, 1990). While 72% of the comprehensive university faculty members reported that the number of publications was "very or fairly important" for granting tenure in their departments, 60% reported having published zero or one to five articles in their entire careers. It is clear that faculty members at SCUs are publishing more than they did decades ago. It is equally clear that even now the rate is low.

What Counts: Reconsidering Scholarship

Most SCU faculty members publish at modest rates. How do they spend their time when they are not teaching? Are critics right to say that too many faculty members are pretentious, lazy, and wasteful (Lewis, 1997; Mandell, 1977)? Faculty members at SCUs (and of course at other nonresearch university institutions) spend their time in a number of productive ways. This is not obvious in the research on faculty productivity, because the nonresearch forms of faculty activity have resisted easy conceptualization and measurement. Socialized in the research model, faculty members themselves have often limited what "counts" to published research. During the past 20 years, Boyer and others (see Boyer, 1990; Johnston, 1998) have led a concerted effort to classify faculty activities within a reconceptualized view of scholarly productivity.

At the 1932 meeting of the American Association of Teachers Colleges, Ambrose L. Suhrie, who held the title of professor of teachers-colleges and normal-school education at New York University, gave a paper in which he argued that some instructors at normal schools and teachers colleges were being pressured to demonstrate scholarly productivity in unproductive ways. He said there was a fetish for pseudo-research that had led to dull books, worthless statistics, inane judgments, and raw, unseasoned conclusions. He told the assembled teachers college presidents that if they were guilty of encouraging such material they "should be solemnly warned by the President of this Association to mend [their] ways" (Suhrie, 1932, p. 60). The faculty member who was an expert on a topic and had something

unique to say should publish. Other faculty members had other legitimate professional activities for which they should be credited. Suhrie gave as examples:
- Taking expertise to communities as a counselor or consultant
- Developing textbooks and materials, translating difficult material for students to understand
- Developing the curriculum so that courses become integrated in ways that better educate students

Almost 60 years later, Ernest Boyer (1990) argued that too much emphasis was placed on a single version of scholarly productivity: the production of peer-reviewed journal articles and books. Boyer did not demean this form of scholarship, but he considered it to be only one form of scholarship, the *scholarship of discovery*. Boyer thought there were at least three other forms of scholarship that should be "counted." In the *scholarship of application*, scholars use their expertise to help solve practical educational, economic, environmental, and other societal problems. The *scholarship of integration* pertains to the efforts to summarize, conceptualize, and critique bodies of existing research across discipline and subdisciplines. Finally, in the *scholarship of teaching*, scholars find the best ways to present ideas and measure the effects of educational interventions. Boyer knew that getting attention to these "new" forms of scholarship (i.e., getting them to count) would require the development of ways to measure and recognize them. He asked, only in part rhetorically, whether the American system of higher education was ready for multiple models of success.

Since Boyer's report was published there have been many efforts to develop his ideas. Braxton and Del

Favero (2002) examined the availability of publication outlets for Boyer's four classes of scholarship. Outlets for all four were available, but outlets for some forms of publication (especially teaching and application) were more available in some disciplines than in others. They also found that the impact factor (an index of the degree to which other scholars cite material) for the scholarship of teaching journals was very low compared to that for scholarship of discovery outlets in the same disciplines. The conclusion of their paper was that alternative means for assessing the scholarships other than discovery are needed. It may also be that within some disciplines the pedagogical journals are not well known. It is also possible that the natures of the scholarships are fundamentally different. For example, teaching innovations may not invite subsequent citations in the same way scholarship of discovery does. Also, the networking of scholars in teaching may be different from research networking, relying less on publication and more on email, meetings, and workshops.

When the Boyer report was published in 1990 there was considerable focus on his argument that the expanded version of scholarship would prove to be especially helpful to faculty members outside the research university sector. For faculty members at institutions struggling to determine mission and appropriate means for evaluating faculty work, the new way of thinking about scholarship would be a boon (Leatherman, 1990). Research by Pellino, Blackburn, and Boberg (1984) conducted before the publication of Boyer's book suggests that he was right. Pellino et al. found that faculty members at a variety of types of

institutions perceived the existence of six different categories of scholarly activity:
• Professional editing and reviewing
• Research and publication
• Artistic expression
• Innovations in teaching and institutional service
• Community service
• Pedagogy (course development, acquiring new information to be taught, curriculum revision)
They found that faculty members at research universities rated research and publication as most important but at all other types of institutions, scholarship as pedagogy was rated highest in importance.

The scholarship of teaching and learning does seem to offer faculty members at comprehensive universities a particularly useful way to be productive. It combines features of traditional research and publication activities with an explicit concern for students and teaching. Have SCU faculty members used this area as an outlet for scholarly activity? Has their involvement in the scholarship of teaching increased since 1989? Heidi Buchanan and I recently looked at these questions (Henderson & Buchanan, 2006b). We identified teaching-oriented journals in four disciplines: chemistry, marketing, psychology, and sociology. We examined the institutional affiliation of the authors in these journals for the years 1977 or 1979, 1990, and 2001, categorized by Carnegie classification (using the classification of the institution at the time of publication). We did the same for a research-oriented journal in each discipline. We also looked at involvement on the journals' editorial boards. We found that while authors and editors from SCUs were almost completely absent from the research journals, they were common in the pedagogical journals. Although there had been some increase in involvement over the time period studied (as indicated by published articles and membership on editorial boards), SCU faculty had already been involved substantially by 1977.

Another distinction about types of scholarship is useful in the SCU context. The traditional forms of scholarship, the production of books, articles, creative works of art and music, textbooks, or review can be called *productive scholarship*. Productive scholarship involves the creation of peer-reviewed works in a specialized area. It makes the scholar's knowledge base deeper but narrower. Most productive scholarship fits into Boyer's category of discovery, although some productive scholarship may be integrative. The motivation for productive scholarship may be intellectual curiosity, but it may also be what Savage (2003) calls *forced productivity*, work that is produced in order to attain tenure, a promotion, or the next raise or job.

As we have seen, only a minority of SCU faculty members are regularly and continuously involved in productive scholarship. Even with Boyer's expanded definition of scholarship with the requisite peer review of teaching- or service-related activities, only a minority of SCU faculty members are involved. However, all faculty members should be involved in a type of scholarship that would not "count" within the traditional forms of scholarly productivity. For want of a better term, this other kind of scholarship can be called *consumatory* (using "consume" in its dictionary meaning of "absorb"). It is similar to what Daly (1994) calls *aggregative scholarship*. In their consumatory scholarship, all faculty members should be reading the scholarly literature, attending professional meetings and workshops, obtaining relevant practical experiences in the field when appropriate, participating in online discussions, and generally maintaining the role of an active learner. Consumatory scholarship is and should be broader than productive scholarship, is unlikely to be systematically peer reviewed, and is as likely to pertain to teaching and service as it is to traditional forms of research. It is most likely to be motivated by intellectual curiosity and the desire to disseminate knowledge in forms that are understandable to nonspecialists (including undergraduate students).

Accounting for how faculty members at SCUs spend their time beyond the 9 or 12 hours a week for 30 weeks a year they spend in the classroom is of the same order of difficulty as accounting for all the matter in the universe. Much of that unaccounted time is spent in activities related to scholarly consumption rather than to scholarly productivity. There are probably ways to better account for some consumatory scholarship than have been used to date (e.g., portfolios provide options for reading logs, lists of experiences, etc.), but consumatory scholarship is unlikely to be peer reviewed in the same ways as are the products of traditional scholarship.

It seems obvious that SCU faculty members can benefit from a vision of scholarship broader than traditional views. Yet some scholars remain unconvinced it will take hold. Bogue and Aper (2000), for example, think that the broader version of scholarship might be accepted in applied areas such as nursing, business, and education. But "the extent to which the modern college and university will welcome and recognize such differentiation in the work of the faculty is a current leadership challenge" (p. 165). Daly (1994) thought it unlikely that scholars trained to be disciplinary researchers would take to low-status pedagogical research that also was unlikely to be rewarded at most universities. Bender (2005) found that faculty members at some institutions report that efforts in the scholarship of teaching and learning (SoTL) are not considered research (i.e., they do not "count") and are not sufficiently rewarded (see also Wright, 2005). Certainly the problems of status (see Chapter 3) represent a major barrier to the acceptance of a new perspective on scholarly activity. However, there is growing interest in SoTL (see Atkinson, 2001; Badley, 2003; Glassick, Huber, & Maeroff, 1997; Huber, 2001; Hutchings & Shulman, 1999; Johnston, 1998; Schon, 1995), and its institutionalization in the form of online journals (the *Journal of the Scholarship of Teaching and Learning*, http://titans.iusb.edu/josotl/ and *Mountain Rise*, http://mountainrise.wcu.edu/), suggests that hope is warranted. Bender argues that SoTL work will become less marginalized as accreditation agencies and other outside groups (e.g., legislators) put increasing pressure on institutions to provide assessments indicative of positive student learning outcomes.

Conclusion: Do Interesting Things

New faculty members who want to earn the rewards of an academic life in terms of tenure, promotion, and merit pay face the problem of determining what will count toward attaining those rewards. They are likely to have been socialized in their graduate education into the model that says publishing in peer-reviewed journals and attaining research grants are what count. Even the rhetoric at many places outside the research university would lead the new faculty member to believe only those things count. I have known many new faculty members at SCUs who believed their futures were tied to being able to put together impressive résumés of endless published research articles. While I was preparing this chapter, I spoke with a senior faculty member in an applied field who was talking about those naïve junior faculty members who were advocating Boyer's multiple forms of scholarship as a basis for their department's faculty evaluation procedures. The senior faculty member commented that they were not "getting it." The "it" according to the senior faculty member was that nothing short of numerous refereed articles was going to suffice for tenure and promotion. I was stunned by this rhetoric in the face of the reality of the modest research productivity of the average faculty member at an SCU (including that particular senior faculty member). A few individuals at SCUs may be able to obtain the grant support to provide the physical facilities, personnel, and release time from teaching duties to allow high levels of research productivity, but the available data suggest they are rare indeed.

The good news is that faculty members at SCUs can and do get involved in many interesting scholarly activities. Included are traditional research and publication at modest levels. Moreover, even within the category of traditional research, SCU faculty members can be accorded a degree of freedom not available at research universities (Vanderstaay, 2005). New faculty members at SCUs should not feel they have to produce great quantities of refereed journal articles to be successful. They should feel free to engage in traditional scholarship that focuses on quality rather than quantity, research that may be risky in its innovation and creativity, rather than being paradigmatic or programmatic. Their product might be a long-term empirical research, a series of minor studies with students, or a thoughtful book. They should feel free to engage in research that involves undergraduate students at all stages in the process. New faculty members who hear tales of the importance of large quantities of traditional publications should investigate the reality. The citation indexes and other databases can help them determine whether the rhetoric and the reality match at their own institutions.

Perhaps more important, faculty members at SCUs should be able to engage in a wide range of scholarly activities. Reward systems must be changed. What "counts" should be doing interesting things. There are signs of change. O'Meara's (2005) survey of chief academic officers (CAOs) indicates that more than two-thirds report modifications in their institutions' reward systems over the past decade to incorporate multiple forms of scholarship. CAOs at masters institutions (comprehensive universities) were the most likely to report such changes.

The scholarship of application fits nicely into SCUs' missions and traditions of economic, educational, and cultural service to their regions. Even more central to the mission and tradition of SCUs is involvement in the scholarship of teaching and learning. Many disciplines have respected peer-reviewed publication outlets for thoughtful, well-documented innovations in teaching and learning. All SCUs should be developing ways to assess the various forms of scholarship. National models are being developed that should aid in those efforts. Faculty members should be encouraged to emphasize different forms of scholarship at different points in their careers. Perhaps most important of all at SCUs, faculty members need to be engaged in serious consumatory forms of scholarship. It is essential that they have broad knowledge of their disciplines that can be used in teaching and service activities. If the faculties and administrations at SCUs can get beyond the status problems that have so often led to low individual and institutional self-images, they can use the broadened vision of scholarship to their advantage, to the advantage of their students, and to the advantage of their communities. These activities are more likely than specialized research to build an institution's reputation, even if they do not increase national prestige (Brewer, Gates, & Goldman, 2002; Park, 1996).

5 Academic Life at SCUs

In the foreword to a book aimed at new faculty members, Schuster (1999) identified four trends in the academic workplace that will influence faculty life in the 21st century:

- The changing nature of teaching, especially the use of technology in new approaches to teaching
- The intensifying pressure for faculty members to be more productive in instruction (teaching more courses and students) and scholarship (publishing more and getting more grants)
- The changing demographic makeup of the faculty, including the aging of faculty members (who are not necessarily retiring), and increasing numbers of part-time faculty
- A trend toward more faculty appointments being full-time but not on tenure track

All four of these trends are apparent at SCUs. In the coming decades many faculty members will retire and many will be hired, and the nature of academic life will not necessarily stay the same. The adaptation to these trends offers special challenges to all faculty members at SCUs, especially for those hired most recently. This chapter focuses on the nature of academic life at SCUs as it is at the beginning of the 21st century. I begin with a description of the faculty and then briefly discuss the four components of academic life most on the minds of individual faculty members: teaching, service, research, and collegiality. Toward the end of the chapter I stress the situation of the new faculty member and some special problems faced by all teachers at SCUs. (See the Appendix for an annotated bibliography of books that provide detailed how-to advice to new and established faculty members.)

Faculty Cohorts at SCUs

Who are the faculty members at SCUs? According to federal data (U.S. Department of Education, National Center for Education Statistics, 2003), there were 83,000 full-time and 48,400 part-time faculty members at public comprehensive universities. The American Association of State Colleges and Universities (AASCU), of which most SCUs are members, estimates that there are more than 3 million students in their member institutions, more than 56% of the students at four-year colleges and universities. According to the National Center for Education Statistics (NCES), about 70.3% of SCU full-time faculty members hold doctorates (as compared to 72.7% for public research and 69.1% for private research universities, 62.1% for private comprehensives, and 60.7% in private liberal arts). Three-quarters of the faculty members at SCUs are between ages 40 and 64, 62% are male, 83% are white (among part-time faculty members at SCUs, 86% are white, 47% are male, and 22% have a doctorate). Full-time faculty members report working an average of 52.4 hours per week. How are faculty members at SCUs spending their time? Reports (U.S. Department of Education, NCES, 2003) about the portions of time spent on various academic activities are presented in Table 5.1 along with comparable data from faculty members at research and liberal arts institutions. Also included in the table are reported preferences for time spent in each area. The data in Table 5.1 show that faculty members at research universities report spending less time on teaching and more on research than SCU faculty members. Faculty members at SCUs report spending slightly less time on teaching and more time on research than their counterparts at liberal arts colleges. At all three types of institutions, faculty members would prefer to be spending a little less time on teaching and more on research and professional development.

The numbers in Table 5.1 are informative, but they do not reveal the qualitative characteristics of SCUs faculty members. The most extensive research on the portion of the academic labor market represented by SCUs is Finnegan's (1993a, 1993b, 1997). According to Finnegan, the characteristics of faculty members at teaching institutions have been largely unstudied. The conceptual emphasis in the research literature on faculty labor markets has been almost exclusively on prestige. The general view of how faculty members obtain jobs has been that doctoral graduates of research universities are matched up with programs of similar prestige (by some unspecified mechanism that continues to involve networks of scholars that once was known as the "old boys system"). Less competent graduates of research universities and those from less prestigious research universities get jobs, if they get them at all, in institutions farther down the prestige hierarchy.

Table 5.1.
Mean Self-Reported Actual and Preferred Proportion of
Time Spent on Academic Activities by Institutional Type

Portion of time spent on:	Type of Institution		
	SCUs	Research Universities	Liberal Arts Colleges
Teaching			
Actual	63.0%	45.9%	65.4%
Preferred	57.0%	42.3%	59.7%
Research & Scholarship			
Actual	11.0%	25.9%	8.1%
Preferred	18.8%	32.8%	15.9%
Professional Growth			
Actual	4.5%	3.5%	4.2%
Preferred	7.7%	6.5%	7.8%
Administration			
Actual	12.8%	7.2%	9.5%
Preferred	7.5%	7.2%	9.5%
Consulting & Service			
Actual	8.5%	11.6%	6.9%
Preferred	9.0%	11.2%	7.6%

Source: U.S. Department of Education, National Center for Education
Statistics (2003)

Finnegan (1993a, 1997) questions this simplistic
view. She argues that some prospective faculty members
opt out of the prestige rat race. They enter the labor
market intent on finding positions that are not tied to
the publish-or-perish mentality or some other negatively
perceived aspect of the research university. Her argument is that the faculty members who populate the
comprehensive universities are *not* mostly Ph.D. holders
who were in the back of the line for jobs at the research
universities and who had to settle for whatever they

could get: "Some faculty, not merely the cast-offs of prestigious institutions, want to make a commitment to a mission of access and teaching" (Finnegan, 1993a, p. 653). Elsewhere she says prospective faculty members at comprehensive universities (as well as those who seek jobs in the liberal arts sector)

> are motivated to continue in their institution or sector by the type of students they encounter, the institutional community they find, the freedom to pursue eclectic research projects, and the institutional emphasis on teaching. These factors are essential components of their professional lives and are more important than smaller teaching loads, better pay, and the pressure to publish. (Finnegan, 1997, p. 347)

Based on data collected in the 1980s, Finnegan (1993a, 1993b) identified three cohorts of 40 faculty members from two comprehensive universities (one private and one public). The first cohort, what she called the "Academic Boomers," was made up of those who were hired at comprehensive universities before 1972. In Finnegan's samples these faculty members had been first-generation college students from working- and middle-class families and were often first-generation Americans. They usually got the idea of teaching from a favorite professor and wanted to teach first-generation-college, working-, and middle-class students like they had been. Hired at a time when comprehensive universities were having difficulty finding professors who had doctorates, many started their careers with only a master's degree and finished the doctorate later or not at all. Most members of this cohort were happy to be working in the comprehensive university sector.

Finnegan's (1993a, 1993b) second cohort, the "Brahmins," were hired between 1972 and 1982 when academic jobs were scarce. Most of these faculty members came from middle-class homes in which at least one parent had been to college. They had typically attended a selective undergraduate college and received a doctorate from a major research university. The Brahmins respected research and liked doing it, but felt that the comprehensive university did not give them the resources they needed to carry on a systematic program of research. Brahmins tended to be unhappy about their view of themselves as scholars and their lives of heavy teaching of sometimes less than enthusiastic students.

Finnegan's (1993a, 1993b) third cohort, the "Proteans" (a word play on their adaptive qualities), was hired after 1982 when the job market opened up a little in some traditional fields. Comprehensive universities, especially the public ones, as the fastest growing segment of higher education, were starting new applied programs that required additional faculty members. This cohort is much more diverse than the other two, with more women, more minorities, and more individuals with undergraduate degrees from nonelite institutions. According to Finnegan, many of the Proteans, like the Boomers, came to the comprehensive university gladly, because they liked the mix of teaching and scholarship offered there. They did not want to be caught up in the prestige game of publish-or-perish. When they encountered difficulty finding full-time jobs, they picked up part-time teaching that allowed them to acquire teaching experience that prepared them for the kinds of jobs that eventually became available.

Although Finnegan's work is based on a very limited sample, I believe it captures some very important features of the faculties at SCUs since the 1960s. I suspect that the precise years for Finnegan's cohorts differ a little from discipline to discipline (e.g., there were probably Brahmins hired at the end of her Boomer period in already overly subscribed disciplines, especially in the arts and sciences). Where are they now? Finnegan's Academic Boomers are just about all gone. The youngest are now over 65 and some may be hanging around campus, but not in large numbers. Finnegan's youngest Brahmins are middle aged and many are nearing the end of their careers. The Proteans dominate the SCU campus of today (along with an unnamed cohort or two that followed them). My own view is that the research orientations of the Brahmins and of the administrators who hired them in an attempt to buttress the prestige of their institutions have left a durable legacy. The data I present in Chapter 4 on changes from the 1950s to the 1990s in publication rates at SCUs suggest that the rhetoric about the importance of SCU faculty members being active publishers had an effect. Publication rates at SCUs went from near zero to modest amounts and have remained there. But the rhetoric surrounding the emphasis on publishing heated up well beyond the reality. Proteans and those who followed them have kept the rhetoric alive. In her interviews, Finnegan (1993a) found that some Proteans felt misled when they discovered that scholarship was required for promotion at the comprehensive universities. Often Proteans conduct pedagogical and applied research. A significant number of SCUs have looked to Boyer's (1990) expanded version of scholarship to try to reconcile the rhetoric and the reality (see Chapter 4).

Finnegan's work contains a sharp critique of the research on academic labor markets, but also tells us about how little we know about academic life in the SCUs. She sees a bias among higher education researchers: "We rate faculty who pursue research as significantly more important, more liberated, more autonomy bearing, and more professional than those who primarily teach" (Finnegan, 1997, p. 353). Finnegan claimed the emphasis on prestige and publishing is a major limitation of research on higher education faculties:

> Rather than continue to foster a systemic model based on status attainment should we not be more concerned with the attributes and properties of knowledge that we are communicating within the sectors and therefore with what we are producing or reproducing in our classrooms as a result of this perspective? . . . Our definitions of quality must be reconsidered. (p. 355)

She went on to point out that: "As long as we continue to limit our investigations to the prestige system with its affiliate variable, professional productivity, we restrict our interest in other elements of faculty life, such as the motivations related to teaching" (p. 356).

In his extensive study of academic life in the 1980s, Clark (1987) described the institutional culture at comprehensive universities as "weak." At research universities the ideal "academic person" is someone who does exciting research, can convey that excitement to students, and has national stature. Academics at comprehensive universities have nothing so coherent with which to identify. Instead, the comprehensive university professor is saddled with local, not cosmopolitan, activities. A "good" comprehensive university professor respects students, knows the discipline, is an enthusiastic teacher, and dabbles with some research interests. What constitutes an ideal is pulled toward the local, including teaching and campus politics. In interviews with faculty members Clark found some of his least content respondents at comprehensive universities. They knew they were no longer at teachers colleges, but they were not at "real" universities either. Because they did not feel good about their universities, they often felt they were underemployed.

Clark's research is colored by a research university bias (see Finnegan, 1994). The "logic of the profession" from Clark's perspective is based on the importance of one's academic discipline, not the importance of students: "The perils of student-centeredness are greater than the dangers of professional dominance" (Clark, 1987, p. 273). Students lead faculty members away from expertise and advanced knowledge. Clark fails to see that some faculty members have chosen to work at comprehensive universities; they were not just *stuck* there. Whereas recognition and respect at the major research university comes from disciplinary peers, faculty members at comprehensive universities (and liberal arts colleges) often look to students for recognition and respect. That may not make sense to Clark, but for those who are interested in the problems of teaching and learning as intellectual challenges and see dealing with those challenges as rewarding, it is the singleminded pursuit of research in the university context that makes little sense.

We do not know about the cohorts that have entered the SCUs since Finnegan did her research. I suspect that most faculty members at SCUs still can be characterized as Proteans. Although there is evidence that graduate programs still do a poor job of preparing prospective faculty members for jobs outside the research university sector (Adams, 2002), graduate students may be more aware now that jobs like those their mentors have are scarce. Finnegan's (1993a, 1993b) research on comprehensive university faculty cohorts needs to be replicated. For many new faculty members at SCUs the limits of their training still become clear very quickly. Daly (1994) put it succinctly: "Most newly minted Ph.D.s are well trained for the life of scholarship which only a few will in fact pursue, and poorly trained for the life of teaching which awaits most of them" (p. 49).

The Components of the Academic Life

New faculty members have a lot to learn (Lucas & Murry, 2002). They have to become acculturated to their disciplines, to the profession, to their institutions as types, and to the particular institution where they are employed. Across institutional types and disciplines, the typical way faculty members are held accountable is to examine performance in teaching, service, and research. Usually not in formal institutional documents is a fourth, fuzzy, category called collegiality. Included in this fourth category may be friendliness with colleagues, positive relations with students outside the classroom, a sense of the degree to which the faculty member is a team player, positive relations with administrators, the willingness to do one's share of chores, and a host of even less concrete characteristics such as honesty, integrity, and warmth. All four categories are important in the academic life of any type of university. (See Chapter 4 for more detail on research.) I treat each of the areas briefly with particular attention to how they might apply differently at SCUs. (More details on each category are contained in the many books available to faculty members annotated in the Appendix.)

Teaching at SCUs: Teaching That Develops Talent

SCUs are *teaching institutions*. What does that mean? It means that faculty members teach more. "More" may be defined in terms of credit hours, teaching load, number of students, or a mixture of indicators. It also means that teaching counts more, or at least that it should count more, toward receiving tenure, promotions, and merit pay increases. Throughout higher education there have been complaints about the degree to which teaching counts. Often it has been assumed that good teaching could not be meaningfully judged; therefore, there was no predictive power in knowing how well someone taught beyond some minimal level of basic competence. Because all but the most inept could attain that basic minimum, everyone was equal on teaching. As a result, in tenure, promotion, or merit decisions, other factors, particularly research records or collegiality provided the only information that discriminated one faculty member from another (Park, 1996).

At teaching institutions students are more likely to be in smaller classes from the freshman year on and they are more likely to be taught by full-time faculty members, rather than by graduate assistants or adjuncts. That does not, however, mean that at a teaching institution the teaching is necessarily more effective or even different. Lecture or some modified form of lecture remains the staple of professors at all kinds of institutions. One other indicator of the centrality of teaching at a university might be the presence of some sort of center for teaching excellence where faculty members can get help to improve their teaching. I do not know of hard data, but I suspect that perhaps a higher percentage of SCUs have created teaching centers; but at all kinds of universities, such centers tend to disappear or get downsized when money is tight.

Astin (1985) argues that colleges and universities have a much better track record in recognizing and rewarding talent than in developing it. Our most prestigious institutions are those that have the most selective admissions criteria. Even the mega-universities have developed honors colleges within the larger campus that contain a relatively small group of highly selected students. They attract students who have been called *prelearners* (Sperber, 2000), students who are independent learners. Faculty members need to do little but point them in the right direction to get them to learn what the average student requires some help with. While all SCUs have students like this, one of the distinctive characteristics of the SCUs is their willingness to deal with less well-prepared students. Many SCU students do not come into college with the academic skills and attitudes that will allow them to benefit from whatever kind of teaching they encounter. The "active" in active learning cannot be dredged up totally from within as it can be with the most advanced high school graduates.

Since the 1970s, the characteristics of teaching that are more likely to intellectually engage students in meaningful ways have become increasingly apparent. There is no simple set of teaching strategies that will turn passive students or teachers into dynamic teaching and learning machines. I leave the mechanics of teaching methods to the advice books summarized in the Appendix, but I do want to say some things about what are the most important characteristics of good teaching for SCU students.

Cognitive psychologists have known for some time that learning that leads to long-term retention and the ability to use knowledge in new situations involves making meaningful connections. Students learn for the long term when they are able to make connections between what they already know and what is to be learned (Bransford, Brown, & Cocking, 1999; Lambert & McCombs, 1997). It is almost impossible to remember what you do not understand. When you understand something you remember it or are able to reinstate it with minimal effort. It follows that the most effective forms of teaching are those which help students to actively make connections between what they know and do not know. Tagg (2003) argues that while universities have touted teaching innovation, their faculty members and students consistently stick to what he calls "the Instruction Paradigm." In the Instruction Paradigm, students are out to get a GPA and a diploma. They do not expect to work hard or for very long. In the contrasting "Learning Paradigm," the goal of the student is to learn. Learning is the outcome of long, hard work on meaningful tasks, often in concert with other students. Examples of the kind of learning environment in the Learning Paradigm include service-learning, problem-based learning, and guided student research.

For most students the lecture is not the ideal environment for meaningful learning. Especially when the class is large, the instructor cannot easily help students make meaningful connections between what they know and do not know. Spence (2001) claims that human beings are fantastic learners. They learn such complex acts as language. Yet traditional classroom teaching cannot be done effectively (Spence points out that there is no market for teachers like there is for researchers, because no one is really that good at producing learning outcomes). He argues that professors should stop trying to be teachers and become designers of learning environments instead. Part of the problem we have in thinking about teaching and learning is that professors and their students, like Spence, tend to think that teaching occurs within the walls of the classroom. That has never been so. The old notion that a student should be spending two to three hours outside class for every hour in class reflected the belief that more learning should be going on outside the class. The effective teacher plans what students will be doing back in the dorm, in the library, with a group of classmates, or in the lab or field. In the classroom the teacher can connect, explain, demonstrate, stimulate, question, evaluate, and occasionally inspire, but cannot do the student's learning. Spence is correct that in some sense, students can only learn one-on-one or alone, but he goes too far. The classroom can be one piece of an instructor's design for learning. The time in the classroom can be used to do many things. Much learning, however, has to be done outside the classroom.

Service: Engagement in the University and the Larger Community

For many faculty members at SCUs, service is the second most prominent component of their jobs. Service has a rich history in the normal school roots of many of the SCUs. There are three major kinds of service: institutional, disciplinary, and community. Institutional service at its most mundane involves the chores that have to be done in order for any organization to function smoothly. New faculty and staff have to be hired, the curriculum needs to be reviewed, textbooks have to be chosen, tenure has to be recommended, and parties need to be planned. Despite the fact that the vast majority of institutional service duties take up a very small percentage of faculty members' time over a calendar year, those duties often are perceived as onerous and time sapping. They also are very low in status. New faculty members are warned not to get too involved in service. Typical advice is to do something to put down on your record, but nothing that will distract from more important tasks. In addition to keeping time commitments down, low institutional service can help avoid negative interactions with your seniors who can later bring up problems at tenure and promotion meetings (e.g., Schwartz is not a team player, is too narrowly focused, or is a prima donna). Older faculty may use service on committees as a means for making up for low productivity in other areas. Despite the low status of most institutional service, there are tasks that are extremely important. Perhaps the most important are those that involve the hiring and retaining of faculty members. The ultimate institutional service is to become an administrator. Administrative duties inevitably require sacrifices in the teaching and research areas that can have long-term effects on a faculty member's career development.

Disciplinary service has more status and at SCUs has the potential to convey considerable status. Disciplinary service consists of becoming involved in the working of an organization in one's discipline at a regional or national level. It may mean serving as a peer reviewer for journals or meetings, serving on an editorial board, helping organize and conduct conferences, helping with recruitment, or many other chores for which professional organizations rely on volunteer help. Disciplinary organizations may be research, teaching, or service oriented. If the organization has some status within the discipline, this form of service may give a faculty member some standing that will "count" on the home campus. If it involves traveling and getting to know other faculty members, especially those from prestigious institutions, it can make the participant more of a cosmopolitan than ordinarily would be the case. The kinds of disciplinary organizations that SCU faculty members are most likely to become involved in are those that have a pedagogical orientation (e.g., in my field, The Society for the Teaching of Psychology) or student orientation (e.g., honorary societies).

The third kind of service has been renamed *engagement* in many quarters. This kind of service involves faculty members applying their disciplinary expertise to problems and issues in the community. This kind of service is probably more common at SCUs than at research universities, liberal arts colleges, or private comprehensive universities. Faculty members at research universities are too busy on larger stages and those at liberal arts and private colleges are less likely than those at public institutions to see engagement as an individual or institutional requirement. Also, because of the applied orientation of SCUs, they are more likely to have faculty members in programs that provide applied expertise in areas like education, business, health services, criminal justice, or applied engineering. Many SCUs have developed centers that provide consulting and applied research expertise for their regions.

Research

Because research is such a complex and contentious issue at SCUs, I have included a separate chapter on it (Chapter 4). For present purposes, I will just say research at SCUs is more likely to be applied or pedagogical than basic in many disciplines. Research that would not "count" at research universities does count at SCUs. Research is likely to be better rewarded and recognized than it is supported (with facilities, time, funds). As I tried to make clear in Chapter 4, the importance of traditional research, in terms of its centrality to academic life, looms much larger in the minds of SCU faculty members than in reality.

Collegiality

Collegiality has multiple meanings in the context of academic life. However, in one way or another, it has to do with the ability of a faculty member to get along with others. Some faculties have used collegiality, formally or informally, as the fourth leg of the faculty performance stool. The American Association of University Professors considers this practice to be dangerous and inappropriate (AAUP, 2001). The AAUP position is that it is redundant to add collegiality as an additional criterion to teaching, research, and service because to the degree to which relationships with colleagues should be considered, those relationships already are involved in the assessment of the other three components. The danger the AAUP and others see in the use of collegiality as a criterion in decisions about faculty members is that collegiality will be defined as congeniality and the willingness to "go along to get along." As a means for reinforcing homogeneity in an academic unit, an emphasis on collegiality can threaten academic freedom, especially in the form of dissent from the judgments of administrators and more senior colleagues. In such cases, much may be lost: "Gadflies, critics of institutional practices or collegial norms, even the occasional malcontent, have all been known to play an invaluable and constructive role in the life of academic departments and institutions" (AAUP, 2001, p. 40).

The issues of collegiality, even by the AAUP's standards, are most likely to be involved in issues related to teaching and service. Because SCUs put particular emphasis on teaching and service, collegiality may be more of an issue at SCUs than at research universities. Silverman (2004) has written a how-to book on being collegial that defines collegiality in broad terms, but terms that align it closely with service. For Silverman, *collegiality* includes everything from attending meetings regularly, congratulating colleagues for their accomplishments, avoiding gossip, and mentoring and advising students, to not proselytizing colleagues or students for deeply held religious or ethical beliefs. His book includes long lists of dos and don'ts for the faculty member aspiring to tenure or promotion, most of which potentially fit the SCU context. However, his book also reveals how much potential mischief there is in using collegiality in the evaluation of faculty members.

A Question of Balance

At all kinds of universities, administrators, faculty members, and community supporters would endorse the idea that teaching, research, and service are all important aspects of a faculty member's job. The difficult task faced by the individual faculty member is how to balance those three aspects in a way that is consistent with the expectations of one's colleagues and institution while still maintaining a semblance of a personal and family life. One factor is the ability to manage time, a topic that is addressed in most of the how-to books annotated in the Appendix. In this section, I address some conceptual issues related to the balancing act.

The most commonly cited conflict among teaching, research, and service is between teaching and research. One view held by many of the critics of higher education is that teaching and research conflict because faculty members who are caught up in doing a lot of research do not have time for undergraduates. An opposing view is that it is expertise in research that provides university teachers with the spark and knowledge that characterize the best teachers. It is the researchers who are most excited about their disciplines and want to pass on that excitement to students who are the finest teachers. A third view is that if research interferes with teaching, that is a small price to pay for the advancement of scholarship. Burke (1988) argues that at research universities it is appropriate that students take on a major portion of the responsibility for their own learning rather than relying on professors.

Most surveys of faculty members indicate that they prefer to spend the largest proportion of their time in teaching or on a mixture of teaching and research at all kinds of institutions (e.g., Boyer, 1990; see Table 5.1). Leslie (2002) goes so far as to say that the valuing of teaching is the unifying core value across institutional type. Faculty members value teaching and derive much internal satisfaction from teaching, even to the point of persisting in the face of extrinsic rewards that favor research. A preference for teaching is stronger at comprehensive universities than at research universities, but the difference is one of degree. What is meant by "teaching" is not always clear. A teaching load is usually measured in number of contact hours in the classroom. However, an accurate assessment of time spent teaching can involve hours in classrooms, formal and informal contacts with students, preparation of lecture materials, organizing in-class and out-of-class exercises and exams, grading papers and exams, and other teaching-related work. Estimates of time spent on teaching-related matters vary, but most suggest at SCUs faculty members spend almost two-thirds of their time on teaching, compared to less than half at research universities (see Table 5.1). Given that faculty members report spending more than 50 hours a week working, there is still a substantial amount of time for nonteaching activities.

At SCUs it is not surprising that faculty members would prefer teaching because they are unlikely to have the time and facilities to engage in many kinds of research. Moreover, the missions of SCUs are different from those of the research universities. Offering educational programs to students from a wide array of backgrounds and offering services to the region in the form of educational, scientific, technical, and economic expertise are central to the SCUs' missions.

Despite the reported preferences for teaching and the importance of regional service, research still maintains the peak in the status hierarchy across institutional types. Only partly tongue-in-cheek, van de Berghe (1970) wrote, "teaching is a necessary evil and an annoying distraction from more profitable ventures" (p. 71). There is no term *research load*. Cynics and noncynics see "time to work on my stuff" as the time that is not taken up by teaching and service. *Research* can mean many different things. Included may be research with students that blends into teaching, informal research not directed to any specific product, grant-funded research, and research in consultation with other institutions, businesses, or agencies. Critics have argued that much academic research is of low quality and relevance (see Altbach, 1995). Defenders would argue that the creative process will always have a high miss rate (see Chapter 4).

The high status of research throughout academe exacerbates the tension individuals feel about balancing time given to teaching and research (see Chapter 3). It is a vicious cycle. The more you teach the lower will be your status. The lower your status, the more you will have to teach. "Anything over six hours indicates that you are a poor bargainer or that you belong to a second-rate institution, and anything over nine hours puts you in academic Alaska" (van den Berghe, 1970, p. 80). The balancing problem is further exacerbated by the fact that time spent teaching is negatively related to salary. Fairweather (1996) has shown that at comprehensive universities, higher salaries are earned by faculty members who:
• Teach only graduate students
• Spend more time on research
• Have published more and are publishing at a higher rate
• Obtain externally funded grants

• Spend the least time on teaching-related matters (including time in the classroom and time in preparation for teaching)

The differences in salary demonstrated by Fairweather are substantial, accumulating to hundreds of thousands of dollars over a long career.

What can individual faculty members do to see a balance in teaching and research? One option is to simply capitulate to reality and follow the advice I have heard frequently given by senior faculty: "spend less time on teaching and more on research." It is not clear that doing so is in the long-term best interests of either the faculty member or the institution (see Park, 1996). A relatively constructive way of changing the balance is to get *release time* in order to do more research; one gets released from teaching duties. There is no such thing as release from research because research is what you do on your time and you would never want to be released from it (institutions impose release time from research on adjuncts and full-time, nontenured faculty members). Release time can be difficult to get at SCUs because of the funding formulas common in state institutions (based on relatively high student-faculty ratios). However, there are many strategies for reducing one's teaching load besides formal release time. Van den Berghe's (1970) list of such strategies is old but still valid if taken seriously: teaching small graduate seminars, letting assistants teach, using guest lecturers or videos, teaching the same course repeatedly without changes, teaching large lectures with few assignments or exams to be graded, and many other more creative means; "A judicious combination of . . . [these] methods can whittle down your load to virtually nothing, and win you a reputation as a progressive and effective teacher to boot" (p. 83).

There have been periodic attempts at the institutional level to establish positions weighted heavily toward teaching, even in research universities. Several decades ago, Caplow and McGee (1958) recommended the establishment of positions for *lecturers* who would emphasize teaching over research. In the 1960s and 1970s the Carnegie Foundation funded the development of a new terminal degree, the Doctor of Arts, which was designed to allow graduate students to do pedagogical research instead of basic research in preparation for a teaching career (Glazer, 1993; Richlin, 1993). More recently some universities, including Duke University, have created nontenure-track positions for teachers (Fogg, 2004). Another way of dealing with the teaching-research balance is through job differentiation. A consortium of private comprehensive universities has proposed some methods for helping faculty members develop a balanced approach with flexibility (McMillin & Berberet, 2002). A key notion in their approach was that of the differentiated workload. Faculty members could agree to take on different amounts of teaching, research, and service for the same amount of reward. Moreover, faculty members might have a different balance of teaching, research, and service at different points in their careers. Boyer's (1990) idea of a "creativity contract" follows the same premises.

Wergin (2002) however pointed out the many barriers to differentiated workloads. They include a lack of consistent commitment to differentiation in tenure, promotion and merit pay decisions, the need for pre-tenure faculty to prove themselves in the research arena, resistance by faculty unions, damage to the shared culture of a department, and a reduction in mobility for faculty who do not conduct research. While the notion that workloads could be differentiated is attractive for some reasons (Fairweather, 1996; Leslie, 2002), there are dangers inherent in the concept beyond those warned of by Wergin. One way institutions have de facto differentiated loads is by increasing the number of part- or full-time, nontenure-track appointments. Senior faculty have often encouraged such appointments (intentionally or not) by sloughing off unattractive chores such as teaching introductory courses, remedial courses, or advising (Rice, 2004).

At SCUs faculty members have to develop a balance of activities that somehow coordinates personal preferences and abilities, institutional expectations, and the realities of SCUs as institutions (see Table 1.1). The relative amount of time faculty members spend on activities changes over the course of their careers (Baldwin, Lunceford, & Vanderlinden, 2005). Undoubtedly compromises have to be made. As institutions, SCUs need to provide flexible criteria for tenure, promotion, and merit decisions that will accommodate differentiated workloads between faculty and within faculty careers. Because SCU faculty members do not conduct nearly as much research as faculty members at research universities (see Chapter 4), there is no reason why such accommodations cannot be made. Faculty members who want to do it all should expect to work very long hours. However gratuitous it may seem, time management may be the key. Faculty members who are working in systems with two 15-week semesters have a lot of time when they are not teaching. Even if one teaches summer school, there is time to develop programs of research and service.

Special Problems of New Faculty and Faculty Socialization

Dinham (1999) points out that many faculty members are surprised by the effort required to make the transition from graduate teaching assistant to full-time faculty member. Graduate school may lead students into believing that they are heading for a life of contemplation and research. She says they are surprised to find out that it is teaching that dominates with only islands of research opportunities. This is particularly true of new faculty members at SCUs who find that summers and term breaks are for research, not leisure. Dinham identifies several kinds of problems for new faculty members, including loneliness; the presence of vague, often unspoken expectations; and problems with time management. Menges and Associates (1999) add to those pressures on time (and energy) and isolation the additional problems of general anxiety about survival, the stresses the job puts on life outside academe, and the dissonance many new faculty members face when they find out that as Dinham says, teaching dominates their time, but it is research productivity that is rewarded. In a three-year longitudinal study of 1,700 faculty members, Menges and Associates examined stress in response to teaching, service, research, and annual review. He found that stress tended to go up over time in all four areas for faculty members at the comprehensive university in his study. Those at the comprehensive university reported much more time spent on teaching and that the stress and time spent on teaching did not change over the three years of the study. New faculty members believed they were doing what their institution expected, but also felt they did not get enough corrective feedback and wanted more time for scholarly activities. In a related aspect of this research, Perry, Menec, Struthers, Hechter, Schonwetter, and Menges (1997) found that an important factor in dealing with stress was new faculty members' perceptions of control over teaching activities. Faculty members who believe that they have little control over what happens to them in their jobs tend to become alienated intellectually and emotionally, become cynical, see students as the enemy, become pretentiously arrogant, and feel deep resentment toward their institution. When faculty members felt they were making headway in their teaching, were being rewarded, and were able to secure the resources they needed to teach effectively, they were less stressed and more satisfied with their jobs. Perry et al. compared research university and community college faculty, who have clear job expectations (either teaching or research but not both) with faculty members at liberal arts colleges and comprehensive universities where there are expectations for both teaching and research. Over the first three years of their careers, adjustment was significantly more positive for those at the research university and community college.

New faculty members get socialized into the profession in formal and informal ways (Tierney & Rhoads, 1994). Socialization functions to build loyalty and commitment to the institution. However, new faculty members tend to change the nature of the institution just as they are being changed. An obvious example of this bidirectionality comes from the research ethos that new faculty members brought to the former teachers colleges in the 1960s and 1970s. The latter example also shows how socialization is anticipatory. Prospective faculty members are provided with skills and attitudes starting in graduate school that they carry over to their first jobs. As a report sponsored by AASCU (1999) indicated, this part of the socialization process often creates mismatches. Graduate school mentors often are largely ignorant of the nature of academic positions outside the research university model and thus are in a poor position to help their graduate students learn about the range of possible academic lives available. Once in a new job, a new faculty member's socialization is continued. At initial entry there may be formal orientation activities, but most socialization is informal and haphazard. Traditionally this has been true at all kinds of institutions; however, the lack of coherent socialization may be particularly detrimental for new faculty members at SCUs, because of the lack of knowledge about the difference between SCUs and other institutions. In SCUs that are especially unclear about identity and mission, new faculty members may have little on which to base their understanding of how SCUs work.

Balancing Challenges and Support: A Special Problem of Academic Life at SCUs?

While trying to stay off the turf of those who provide how-to advice on teaching and other faculty activities, there is one more general issue in regard to teaching at SCUs I feel is important. It involves another balancing problem, the problem of challenging students intellectually while supporting them in their efforts to meet high expectations. The balancing of challenge and support is an issue at all types of institutions of higher education.

However, because of their histories and missions, I believe it is a particular problem at SCUs. As far back as the normal school period of many of the SCUs (Herbst, 1989; Holland, 1912/1972; Kent, 1930), there has been a lack of respect from others in higher education and from the general public for the institutions that became the state comprehensive universities. There are numerous reasons for the lack of respect for normal schools, teachers colleges, and comprehensive universities, but a major issue that has haunted these institutions is a perception that students are not sufficiently challenged.

One reason for the lack of intellectual challenge is tradition. As we saw in Chapter 2, the normal schools and teachers colleges were always under pressure to produce teachers and produce them fast. Moreover, the supporters of the colleges in the community wanted their children to receive higher education in easily accessible forms. Too often the result was a campus climate that was not always as intellectual as it might have been. A second, related reason for the lack of intellectual challenge has been that many of the students who have attended SCUs and their predecessors have been less well prepared for college than students who attend more selective public and private four-year universities (see the section in Chapter 6 on unpreparedness). A form of self-fulfilling prophecy is set up wherein professors do not ask very much of their students and they, as a result of a lack of practice, become less able to perform at higher levels. Faculty members may also harbor beliefs about students that strengthen the prophecy. Too often faculty members believe that their students are not very bright and are not capable of getting any brighter. They may attribute student failure to their inherent deficiencies rather than to inadequate teaching methods. Accompanied by concerns about student evaluations of faculty, teachers may make their courses less challenging than they should be.

A third reason for the lack of challenge also comes from the roots of many of the SCUs. From the normal school period on, faculty members at SCUs have been spread too thin. They have frequently been asked to teach courses outside their expertise, or at the margins of their knowledge bases. It is difficult to challenge students in areas in which you are not expert yourself. Faculty members are also spread thin by trying to maintain programs of research and regional service at unreasonable levels. It takes time to challenge students. It means preparing and grading more assignments, reading more books to be discussed, and helping more students who are struggling. At institutions in which the reward system is biased toward research and/or service it is hardly surprising that faculty members hesitate to invest large amounts of time in challenging their students. Finally, faculty members at SCUs may diminish challenge to increase retention of students. Retention and graduation rates tend to be especially low at SCUs (see Chapter 1). Administrators may pressure faculty members, in subtle and not so subtle ways, to make it easier for students to pass. A seemingly more benign but ultimately more destructive form of this cause for low challenge is a concern for student welfare. The concern may be that student self-esteem is fragile or that because so many students at SCUs carry outside jobs, course workloads need to be reduced accordingly. The result is a ratcheting-down of expectations for student academic work.

There are many kinds of good teaching that lead to student learning and development. Good teachers may be stimulating lecturers, masterful discussion leaders, thoughtful critics, designers of interesting experiences, skilled directors of independent research, or wise supervisors of practical field experiences (Brookfield & Preskill, 1999; Fink, 2003; Lee, 2004; McKeachie, 1994; Mirochnik & Sherman, 2002). I believe good teaching of all of these kinds involves significant intellectual challenge. Also characteristic of all these forms of good teaching is support for the challenged student. Good teachers set realistic but high standards for the quantity and quality of student work. They also find effective ways to support students who have been challenged. Four means of providing support are helpful. One is to be available to students. Physical availability is important and less of a problem at SCUs than it is at many research universities, although the increasing use of part-time faculty members is changing availability. More important is psychological availability that is conveyed through genuine interest in student concerns, being willing to say "I don't know, let's find out," learning and using student names, and generally signaling approachability. Another way of supporting challenged students is to pace work requirements. The old schedule of a midterm, a final, and a big research paper due at the end of the semester almost eliminates the possibility of much support. Frequent examinations and shorter writing assignments increase the availability of feedback and support.

A third means of supporting students is to use an overall teaching style that melds challenge and support. The character Kingsfield in the *Paper Chase* (Osborn,

1971) makes for good theater, but that imperious style is not likely to lead to learning for most students. There are real differences between an authoritarian teaching style and an authoritative style. An authoritative style stresses high expectations and firm standards but also stresses two-way communication. Authoritative teachers communicate availability, avoid arbitrary difficulty in tests and assignments, take care not to belittle students, and model appropriate ways for dealing with intellectual challenge without intimidating the novice learner with demonstrations of expertise or the unnecessary use of jargon. Finally, a necessary support for challenge is a willingness to tolerate error. Students need to know that errors are not always fatal and can be a means toward the end of learning.

I argue in Chapter 3 that SCUs will profit from focusing on reputation rather than prestige. An essential component of an improved reputation will come from showing that students are intellectually challenged by the teaching and learning opportunities provided by a university's faculty. The ultimate accountability for SCUs will be found in graduates who are not only competent in their disciplines upon graduation but who are able to continue to develop intellectually over a lifetime.

Conclusion

Academic life at SCUs is different from academic life in major research universities and liberal arts colleges. Although the traditional structure of teaching, research, and service applies to SCUs, the components are mixed in different portions. The faculty member who tries to reproduce the research university recipe at SCUs is likely to be disappointed and unhappy. There are advantages to the SCU mix. In teaching, classes at SCUs tend to be smaller (than undergraduate courses at a research university) and contain a wide range of students from a broad set of backgrounds. The students at SCUs are not, for the most part, prelearners. They need the benefit of teachers who they can get to know, who can provide regular feedback to them, and who are not insulated from them by graduate teaching assistants. The value-added concept applies well to the student experience at SCUs; the best faculty members at SCUs know how to develop talent, not just recognize it. In research, faculty members may get to do less than they would at a research institution, but they should have greater flexibility in topic choice and methodology. There will be less pressure to do grant-driven research. Faculty members in many disciplines will be able to conduct research, not just manage others who do their research for them. Applied research will be welcomed, not just tolerated. In service, faculty members have the opportunity to be involved in meaningful service to a region that often will not have other sources of comparable expertise. On the whole, for the faculty member who is not status driven, the SCU setting has a lot to offer to a balanced academic life.

6 Campus Community

Faculty members at colleges and universities are no more or less committed to their organizations than other professionals are to theirs. Individual faculty members look out for their own interests at about the same rate as any other employees. However, academe is more social in nature than many other endeavors. Also, tenure provides an unusual degree of institutional commitment to the employee and implies a similar degree of reciprocity. It is easy to be cynical about the extent to which faculty members are committed to their institutions. Academics, by training and by disposition, tend to be highly critical. They also tend to be independent and even isolationist in their work habits and attitudes. The image of the ivory tower conveys a sense of separation and isolation from the world. From the perspective of the ivy league, Damrosch (1995) describes the scholar as exile. The super-specialization of the modern academic almost ensures that most faculty members will not always have someone in the same subject area to converse with on campus. Moreover, what Damrosch calls the "scholarly personality" conspires with the reward system to pull faculty members away from teaching and local service. Yet a college campus provides an opportunity for community that is rare in an era in which employees move from job to job and even career to career many times in their lives.

What is communal about a university, particularly a state university? A superficial answer to that question is that the university serves the larger community. But the members of the larger community have ideas about the nature of that service. They want their children and future employees to receive *higher* education. Thus, the university is a community of support, academic and social support for the students. On a residential campus students spend a small portion of their time under the supervision and direction of the faculty. A wide array of other members of the community from the residence hall personnel to the food service workers to the director of intramurals support students. Of course, the university is more than a community of support or it would not differ much from a resort (or at least a summer camp). A university is also a community of scholarship. The overriding value of the university is learning. The community exists to enhance the learning of students by using the learned expertise of the faculty. Included among the students are undergraduate students, graduate students, the regional economic, educational, and cultural communities, and even society at large. It is this broad community of scholarship that most clearly distinguishes the real university from the pseudo-university (Altbach, 2005) of the business and for-profit education worlds.

This is not the place for a detailed sociological analysis of all the aspects of community at SCUs (and I am not capable of such an analysis in any case). Instead, this chapter focuses on some aspects of two subclasses of the university community: students and administrators. I discuss what I think are some important features of these groups at SCUs. I also take a very brief look at two other components of the university community: the staff and intercollegiate athletics.

Students

Some faculty members are fond of saying that there would be no university without the faculty. The implication is that the real reason for the university's existence is to provide the faculty with a place to conduct scholarship. However, at least at SCUs, we know that the reason the state indulges us is that we provide an education for the sons and daughters of the taxpayers. Given the importance of students to the whole enterprise, it is surprising that the systematic study of college students as a group is a relatively recent phenomenon. The work of scholars such as Perry (1970), Astin (1984, 1996) and Pascarella and Terenzini (1991, 1995, 2005) has questioned many assumptions about college students. This section highlights some of what we have found out about students that seems to be of particular relevance to the SCU context.

Student Unpreparedness

Many SCUs are open access, or at least admit a very high percentage of the students who apply. Only high school graduates with the lowest entrance test scores and high school grades are excluded. Sometimes students must successfully complete coursework at a community college prior to admittance. Because SCUs tend to be less selective than many flagship universities or private comprehensive or liberal arts colleges, a perception of many SCU faculty members is that their students are not very good. Faculty members at SCUs who try to talk about students without resorting to inaccurate negative labels often say that SCU students are underprepared.

Pitts, White, and Harrison (1999) interviewed 14 faculty members at two open-admission SCUs about what they called student unpreparedness. Pitts et al. found that all their respondents saw the poor academic preparation of their students as a major problem. The investigators extracted several areas of concern about student preparedness. Faculty members saw many students as poor readers and writers. They also thought many students were not only unprepared but unmotivated. A growing number of students seemed to them to take a passive approach to learning. Students coped with the situation by attributing their difficulties to faculty members who were being unreasonably difficult. They also tended to develop an adversarial relationship with faculty members.

There are a number of important aspects of student underpreparedness that the data from Pitts et al. (1999) do not tell us about. What proportion of students at SCUs are underprepared or undermotivated? What dimensions of individual differences do we need to know about in order to more effectively teach under-prepared students? What the Pitts et al. study shows us most generally is how little we know about SCU students. The next two sections address the available data on student engagement at SCUs and some dimensions of student individual differences that are likely to be useful in helping us improve teaching.

Student Engagement at SCUs

Perhaps the most informative source on what SCU students are doing is the National Survey of Student Engagement (NSSE). The NSSE principles are consistent with the philosophy that the best way to identify the most effective educational practices is to focus on student experiences rather than educational resources or alumni outcomes (which are biased by student entering characteristics; Pascarella, 2001). The NSSE data should be viewed cautiously because participation in the project is voluntary (and by subscription). Further cautions are that the data come from student self-reports, not direct observations of behavior and there may be return rate biases. However, a very wide array of institutions have been involved in NSSE, including many SCUs, and the technical data on their survey instrument is impressive (see the NSSE web site: http://www.nsse.iub.edu).

The NSSE survey is organized around five indicators of student engagement (example contents of survey items are provided in parentheses):

- Level of challenge (number of books and articles read, papers written, experiences in analyzing and synthesizing ideas)
- Active and collaborative learning (making class presentations, working on projects with peers, participating in community service projects, discussing course readings with others outside of class)
- Student-faculty interaction (talking with faculty members about course material or career plans, participating in research with a faculty member)
- Enriching educational experiences (conversing with students of different backgrounds, doing volunteer work, using listservs or chats, studying abroad)

• Supportive campus environment (availability of support services for academic and social life, having positive relationships with other students, staff, and faculty members)

The survey is typically administered to first-year students and seniors.

Detailed results from the latest NSSE surveys are available on their web site (http://www.nsse.iub.edu). I report here what seem to be the clear patterns from NSSE's 2004 survey as they contrast results for SCU students compared to students at research universities and liberal arts colleges (see also Kuh, Gonyea, & Williams, 2005 on the data from 2003). Across indicators, SCU first-year and senior students score at the national average in student engagement. They report levels of academic challenge similar to the responses of students at research universities, but considerably lower than those of students at liberal arts colleges. Most striking is the finding that 74% of first-year SCU students and 69% of SCU seniors report spending less than 16 hours per seven-day week on academic work. Similarly low levels of academic work were reported by students at research universities but not by students at liberal arts colleges. Kuh (2003) points out that these data reveal a "disengagement compact." Students agree to leave faculty members alone to do their own things if the faculty members, in return, do not ask too much of the students. Combined with the fact that most students report getting grades of B and above with this limited effort, it is clear that most students are not rigorously challenged.

On the other NSSE indicators the results are similar. SCU first-year and senior students report scores on active and collaborative learning, student-faculty interaction, and supportive campus environments that are close to those of the students at research universities (near the national average) but scores that indicate much lower engagement than that of students at liberal arts colleges. Most students at all types of institutions report working with other students frequently and report moderate amounts of interaction with faculty members in and out of class. The one exception to this general pattern is for the enriching educational experiences indicator. Students at SCUs and research universities score much lower than liberal arts college students on studying abroad, enrolling in foreign language courses, becoming involved in community service, and having a culminating experience in the senior year.

Overall, the NSSE (2004) data suggest that in terms of student engagement, SCU students' experiences are more like those of the students at large doctoral, research-oriented universities than of the students at liberal arts colleges. At the latter there tends to be an "engagement compact." Umbach and Wawrzynski (2005), using NSSE data, showed that at institutions where faculty members frequently use active and collaborative learning approaches, students are academically challenged and frequently interact with faculty members. Because regional SCUs often market themselves as offering a high degree of student-centeredness, the NSSE results suggest an "engagement gap" between the SCUs' self-images and their students' perceptions.

Student Outcomes

The most comprehensive review of the effects of college on students is provided by Pascarella and Terenzini (2005). Summarizing their earlier work (Pascarella &

Terenzini, 1991) and hundreds of studies done subsequently, they revealed that college does indeed influence student outcomes independent of maturation. Students gain in verbal, quantitative, and subject-matter knowledge, although the changes are surprisingly small in absolute terms. College students also show gains in general intellectual growth that show that they learn how to learn. There is evidence for increases in principled moral reasoning and in the sophistication and breadth of attitudes and values. However, in regard to the relative effects of different types of colleges, there is little evidence of differential effects. There is some indication that the emphasis a college puts on scholarship and learning matters, but whether a student attends a research university, liberal arts college, or SCU seems to make little difference.

In some ways Pascarella and Terenzini's (2005) findings are not very surprising. The differences in what goes on within college type are so great that between type differences are likely to be small. Good teaching and bad teaching (and good and bad learning) occur at every type of institution. Moreover, the bulk of Pascarella and Terenzini's work points out that the NSSE approach to understanding the college experience makes sense. Pascarella and Terenzini sum up the situation in this way: "What a student does during college will generally have a substantially greater impact on his or her subsequent career attainment than where he or she attends college" (p. 525).

Student Individual Differences

The NSSE data and Pascarella and Terenzini's (2005) summary provide group results. But we all know that students differ from each other in many ways. Knowing that students differ on any particular characteristic is useful only when that knowledge leads to differentiated instruction that works. Suppose we know that one student has high intelligence and the other has low intelligence. We have two teaching methods, Method A and Method B, we can use to teach a topic. Using Method A works for the low intelligence student but not for the high intelligence student. Method B works for the high intelligence student but not the low. Therefore knowing a student's intelligence gives us information that allows us to tailor teaching more effectively. Note the assumptions required for a dimension of individual differences. We have to have a reliable, valid measure of the individual difference dimension (one that is reliable for individuals, not just for groups). We need different teaching methods. We need evidence that people at different points on the individual difference dimension respond differently to the teaching methods (the technical term for this is *aptitude-treatment interaction*).

Most SCU faculty members would probably list diversity in ability as a major distinguishing characteristic of SCU students. There is more difference among students within one SCU than between SCUs and other institutions. There are students who could compete with those anywhere (and eventually do) while there also are weak students. Will the dimension of intelligence or general cognitive ability work as a dimension of individual differences that will lead to differentiated instruction? The most common metric for describing individual differences in college students' cognitive ability is the SAT or ACT. Most of the students at SCUs score in the middle range or a little higher on those tests. That tells as much about students' socioeconomic status (SES) levels and the quality of their high schools as anything else. It tells us little about how we should teach them. There is little or no evidence for different instructional methods that work differently for low and high scorers on tests of general ability. Not surprisingly, most methods work better with students high in ability. What other dimensions of individual differences might provide more useful information?

Cognitive styles. Two dimensions of individual differences were studied in the 1950s and 1960s in the hope of documenting aptitude-treatment interactions: field dependence-field independence (FD–FI) and impulsivity-reflectivity (see Sternberg & Grigorenko, 1997, for a summary). Research on the latter focused on young children. Research on FD–FI covered all ages. The basic notion in FD–FI is that some individuals are more influenced in their perceptions and thinking by the surrounding context (FD) than others who are better able to ignore distractions in the wider context (FI). One means of testing individual differences in FD–FI is to have individuals find small pictures hidden in a larger picture (e.g., find the upside down cat among the trees and bushes à la *Where's Waldo?*). An admittedly over-simplified summary of a great deal of research is that FD–FI is related to vocational interests (engineers are more FI whereas social workers tend to be more FD) and some other variables. But I know of no evidence that shows that particular means of instruction work better or worse for FD or FI individuals.

Learning styles. Perhaps the most popular way to conceptualize individual differences has been in the form of some kind of style of learning. Learning styles of students may be packaged in terms of the sensory modalities or channels (e.g., visual versus auditory learners), brain hemisphere dominance (left brainers as logical and analytic and right brainers as holistic and creative), or personality types (introverts versus extraverts, sensors versus intuitors). Again, in an over-simplification of a great deal of research, the problems with conceptualizing and measuring the various kinds of styles have been serious. It turns out to be very difficult to conceptualize learning styles in a way that is theoretically and practically meaningful, reliably measure learning styles, and validate any particular measure of learning styles. Most important, there is little or no evidence for aptitude-treatment interactions, despite claims to the contrary (Dunn & Griggs, 2000).

From the perspective of modern theories of cognition (e.g., Bransford, Brown, & Cocking, 1999), it is not surprising that the learning style approach has not been useful for developing differentiated instruction. We know that students learn best when material is made meaningful in as many ways as possible. If you want students to understand the major causes of World War II or how atomic fission works, you want to engage as many of the students' senses as you can, to involve them in analytic and holistic processing, and generally teach concepts in as many ways as you can think of in as many contexts as you can. Although identifying a particular student's preferred learning styles is likely to be a waste of time, and may be harmful if a student begins to believe, "I only learn through seeing," using varied teaching methods offered by learning-styles advocates can help students process information in varied ways and thus remember it better. Otherwise, the construct of learning styles is of little use in dealing with college students.

Achievement motivation. Several aspects of achievement motivation are related to college outcomes such as GPA and retention. In a meta-analysis of studies, Robbins, Lauver, Le, Davis, Langley, and Carlstrom (2004) examined the relationship of general achievement motivation (the drive for academic success), academic goals (commitment to obtaining a degree) and academic self-efficacy (confidence in the ability to succeed in college) to GPA and retention. All three constructs were predictive of retention, as strongly or more strongly on average as were SES, high school GPA and ACT/SAT scores (but not as strongly as academic-related skills such as time management and study habits). Academic self-efficacy was nearly as predictive of college GPA as high school GPA and more so than test scores, SES, or academic-related skills. Achievement motivation and achievement goals were more predictive of college GPA than SES or academic skills but not as strongly related as high school GPA or test scores.

The Robbins et al. (2004) findings are important; however, we do not know the degree to which they apply in particular to SCUs or other kinds of institutions (Weissberg & Owen, 2005). It also is not clear how susceptible to intervention these constructs are. To what extent can educators influence general drive for success or commitment to obtaining a degree? Moreover, is achievement motivation the cause or effect of success? One achievement motivation-related construct seems to have significant potential for understanding SCU students and has been shown to be influenced by interventions: personal theories of intelligence.

Theories of intelligence. Dweck (2000) has argued that everyone has a theory of how intelligence works. Some are *trait* or *entity* theorists. A trait theorist believes that each person has a certain amount of intelligence, probably determined at birth or soon after. Some people have more general intellectual ability than others. If a trait theorist encounters an intellectual task and cannot do it, it is because he or she simply did not have enough intelligence. There is no use in exerting effort to complete the task. In fact, exerting effort will only reveal one's lack of intelligence. Challenges are to be avoided, because they, too, will reveal inadequacies. In the classroom, the teacher's job is to evaluate the trait theorist and indicate his or her level of intelligence. Other people are *incremental* theorists. Incremental theorists believe that everyone has a certain amount of intelligence at any one time, but intelligence is not a stable entity and more can be obtained. A person obtains more by learning from experiences, especially challenging experiences in which failure is followed by renewed and revised effort with new approaches to the failed tasks. Teachers provide task-relevant feedback and emotional support to help the incremental theorist through the failure experiences, turning those failures into learning opportunities.

There has been no systematic research comparing theories of intelligence of SCU students compared with other students. However, I suspect that many college students are trait theorists. I also suspect that SCUs have more than their share of trait theorists. What good would it do to know? One possibility is that identified trait theorists could receive *reattribution* training. Briefly, reattribution training entails learning to attribute failures to a lack of effort rather than to a lack of ability.

Students can be shown that they can get smarter. We already know that self-efficacy is a powerful predictor of achievement, so it seems that reattribution training could be effective. There also is evidence that students can be trained to attribute difficulties to unstable causes (adjustment to college) rather than to stable causes (lack of ability) with subsequent improvements in academic performance (see Aronson, Fried, & Good, 2002; Wilson, Damiani, & Shelton, 2002). Another implication of the theories construct comes from the fact that faculty members also have theories of intelligence. I am speculating, but I suspect most faculty members are trait theorists. (As indicated earlier, ask faculty members what the quickest way to improve their institution is and they are very likely to say "get better students," a clear sign of trait theories). When faculty members believe their students cannot get smarter, they are unlikely to act in ways that would make the students more intelligent. Reattribution training for faculty members could be interesting.

Other constructs. There are other dimensions of individual differences that appear to hold promise for understanding SCU students. One is the concept of *approach to learning* (Ramsden, 1992; also see Gow & Kember, 1990). Part of the approach to learning is whether the student takes a deep or surface approach to a learning task. Those with a deep approach focus on what the task is about (e.g., what the author of a reading intended) whereas those with a surface approach focus on more superficial aspects of the task (such as the word or sentence level of the text). So many first-year students enter college with a superficial approach, the dimension may not discriminate well, but it seems worth further research. The degree to which a student engages active attention and memory processes is a central issue in cognitive learning theories and could be a useful measure of individual differences with practical implications for learning.

Students: Conclusion

Beyond basic demographics, test scores, and high school GPAs, we have little systematic knowledge of how SCU students differ from students at other kinds of institutions. The NSSE data are helpful, but because students are rating their experiences relative to the institutions they are enrolled in, cross-institutional category comparisons are of limited usefulness. It is possible that most individual differences do not matter, although I find the potential for the theory of intelligence and approach to learning ideas intriguing. It may be that because differences within institutions are greater than differences between institutions, and because good teaching attenuates the role of individual differences, we need not focus on differences but instead focus on individual students. There are important differences in the lifestyles of students at comprehensive universities that have not received enough research attention. Kuh et al.'s (2005) NSSE data indicate that in addition to spending less time preparing for class than students at research universities and liberal arts colleges, students at comprehensive universities (public and private) spend much more time working, commuting, and caring for dependents and less time in cocurricular activities. More needs to be known about the causes and effects of these differences.

Administration

Many ways of thinking about leadership in higher education have been proposed (Birnbaum, 1988). Some of
these approaches represent modifications of business
models. The approach I take here, adapted from
Bergquist (1992), is not. Instead, it reflects the broader
culture in which administrators work. A culture is a
collection of assumptions, beliefs, behaviors, and attitudes that guides much of what its members consider to
be important. Bergquist describes four organizational
cultures. Campuses always have some mixture of two
or more of the cultures, but the administrators are likely
to represent one culture best. I describe each of the
cultures, comment on the kinds of administrators likely
to be found in each culture, and discuss the application
of each culture to the SCU setting.

Collegial Culture

The collegial culture is the culture of the traditional,
stereotypical residential college. It is the culture of
Hollywood's idea of a college with the leafy quadrangle
and tweed-suited professors. The faculty is the central
element of the collegial culture. The programmatic
emphasis is on scholarship as basic research, teaching as
the presentation of disciplinary knowledge, and students
as eager, respectful sponges soaking up the utterances of
the masters. The "good" professor is one who produces
many scholarly publications and who turns out clones
who go on to graduate school where they learn to be
professional scholars and keep the cycle going. The
most highly held values in the collegial culture are
individualism and autonomy. Many of the critiques of

higher education from insiders have come from the collegial culture (e.g., Solomon & Solomon, 1993).

Administrators in the collegial culture have traditionally come from the faculty ranks, "first among equals." By tradition it was important for administrators to come from the faculty because in the collegial culture, faculty members are highly suspicious of the need for administrators of any kind. If they must exist, they need to be respected members of the culture. Faculty members in the collegial culture resent the idea of working for anyone, including a department head, dean, provost, or president. In recent years, even within the collegial culture, administrators are increasingly likely to commit to administration early in their careers and to move from institution to institution before they can gain the respect of faculty members in the collegial culture. Faculty members in collegial cultures tend to give heavy weight to traditional forms of faculty governance such as faculty senates, as a check against administrators. Collegial cultures often have a strong political component.

The collegial culture probably dominates few of the SCUs for at least two reasons. First is that the tradition of most SCUs lies in a history outside the collegial culture (see Chapter 2). The idea that SCUs are teaching institutions conflicts with the collegial culture's emphasis on research productivity. Second, many trends within SCUs over the last few decades work against a traditional collegial culture. One is the trend toward accountability. The strong valuing of autonomy leads faculty members in the collegial culture to resist attempts to be held accountable in terms of teaching load, teaching evaluations, or other measures. In his 1987 study, Clark argued that SCU faculty members were more accepting of authority than those at research universities and liberal arts colleges who largely want to be left alone and go along with administrators who basically leave them alone. Another trend against collegial cultures in SCUs is the emphasis on increasing service to the region, service that requires an outward expression of scholarly activity. Finally, the collegial culture thrives in small settings. The increasing size of many SCUs makes it hard for them to nurture a strong collegial culture.

Although the collegial culture probably dominates few SCUs, it is represented in most, especially within the traditional arts, sciences, and humanities. A positive aspect of the collegial culture presence is that superficial changes in curriculum and other matters are resisted, whether instigated from within or without the institution. The centrality of scholarship within the collegial culture can have a positive influence on the larger institutional values, especially if scholarship is conceived broadly (Boyer, 1990). There are also negative features of the collegial culture at SCUs. One is that it can be very difficult for the collegial culture to aid adaptations to changes in the regional economies and cultures. The slow, conservative, deliberative processes of the collegial culture hinder rapid change. The other negative feature of the collegial culture at SCUs is that faculty members may be constantly receiving mixed messages about what is considered important in the tenure, promotion, and merit systems. Heavy teaching loads and needy students call for an emphasis on teaching while the collegial culture says it is contributions to traditional published scholarship that really count (see Chapter 3). The type of administrator most likely to thrive in the collegial culture is one who has gained the respect of the faculty, particularly administrators who have kept teaching, but especially have kept doing research.

Managerial Culture

The managerial culture is a product of modern business practices being applied to higher education. In the managerial culture, administrators are corporate managers, faculty members are workers, and students are customers. The overriding value of the managerial culture is efficiency. In the managerial culture, faculty members accept the authority of administrators. Whereas tradition is important in the collegial culture, it has no place in the managerial culture. Faculty governance tends to be weak in this culture. Entrepreneurial administrators reap rewards. Bigger is better because of economies of scale.

Bergquist (1992) argues that managerial cultures are common in professional schools but also in community colleges, and private comprehensive universities, especially those that are Catholic. However, managerial cultures have become more common throughout higher education, including in SCUs. Perhaps the clearest sign of their presence is the increasing number of part-time faculty members and faculty members who are full-time but not on tenure track. Such faculty members, who often have come from business or other applied settings, generally have not internalized the values of the collegial culture and are willing to accept administrative authority. Bergquist also argues that whether they are full- or part-time, faculty members in the managerial culture spend little time on campus.

The major positive feature of the managerial culture is its valued efficiency, a quality that may be especially appreciated when institutions face economic downturns.

One negative feature is that scholarship, in its best sense, may be missing in important ways. Learning for learning's sake, creative exploration, and time for reflection may all be seen as inefficiencies. Equally important, the lack of institutional commitment common in the managerial culture is likely to exacerbate the difficulties many SCUs have in establishing institutional identity (see Chapter 3). Administrators who work in the managerial culture may feel more concern for their *next* jobs than the ones they currently hold. Perhaps most important, administrators, faculty members, and students may find institutions dominated by the managerial culture to be relatively uninteresting places to spend their time.

Negotiating Culture

The negotiating culture can roughly be defined as the unionized culture. Its basic values are equity and egalitarianism. In many ways the modern negotiating culture is the result of the breakdown of the traditional collegial culture or a modification of the managerial culture. Bergquist argues that the presence of the negotiating culture becomes more likely under conditions of growing size, decreasing financial support, retrenchment, and faculty alienation. It is unclear whether faculty alienation is a cause or an effect of the negotiating culture.

Middle managers (department heads and deans) are caught in the middle in the negotiating culture. They are neither labor nor management. Thus the administrators faculty members have the most contact with are those who are most detached from the institution's identity. In the negotiating culture, there is likely to be a good deal of red tape and legalism. At SCUs the result is likely to be the presence of a managerial culture among administrators and a highly individualistic culture among faculty members. While individualism is a characteristic of the collegial culture, it is not the same in the negotiating culture, because the bureaucratic and legalistic structures constrain autonomy and do not include the collegial culture's emphasis on scholarship. While the negotiating culture is common at SCUs, it is almost completely unrepresented in the highest status, most collegial campuses in American higher education (e.g., those in the ivy league and the small, highly selective liberal arts colleges). The administrators in the negotiating culture are unlikely to be the first among equals as respected colleagues, but they may be effective, entrepreneurial managers.

Developmental Culture

According to Bergquist (1992), the developmental culture is characterized by its emphasis on teaching and learning rather than on scholarly research. The *developed* in developmental culture are students and faculty members. Bergquist sees the roots of the developmental culture in the work of higher education scholars who were looking for a means of attenuating the deficiencies of the collegial culture (e.g., Astin, 1996; Perry, 1970). However, in some sense, the developmental culture has always been present, especially on the small liberal arts college campuses. Key values in the developmental culture include rationality, planning, and organization. Inclusion, accessibility, and fidelity to institutional mission are emphasized in the developmental culture.

Administrators in developmental cultures are experts and persuaders. They are not paternalistic or managerial. They constantly assess the environment of the institution and reevaluate what their organizations should be doing. They are not only open to change, they initiate it. Unlike managerial administrators, who tend to distance themselves from faculty members and their concerns, administrators in the developmental culture are willing to work closely with the faculty, especially on accountability issues.

The developmental culture is a natural fit for most SCUs, especially those that are not unionized. The emphasis on teaching, learning, and student development is consistent with the emphasis on traditions of teaching and learning at SCUs. The need to be flexible in planning fits the regional service niche of the SCUs. The chief negative feature of the developmental culture is that it puts high demands on administrators. For the administrator at a growing, effective SCU, the institution is greedy indeed and asks administrators to do all and be all. It is unclear whether there are enough sufficiently talented administrators to fill the need.

Staff

The most varied, least researched, and most underappreciated segment of the higher education community is the staff. The staff includes those who admit students; those who provide students with food, housing, and medical care; those who provide extracurricular activities; and those who help them find jobs. Staff members answer the phones, file the records, take care of the grounds, publicize the institution's accomplishments, and pay the bills. Staff members keep in touch with alumni, ask the well-to-do for money, and lobby the legislature. Many staff members belong to their own professional organizations with their own conferences and journals. Despite all the important tasks that staff members perform, information about them and their concerns rarely appears in writings on higher education read by faculty members. They are often ignored by those they serve, including faculty members, students, and the general public.

I will not attempt to educate faculty members at SCUs on the functions of the staff. However, it is important for faculty members, especially new ones, to be aware of and appreciate all the behind-the-scenes personnel who work at SCUs. It also is important to note some differences between faculty members and staff members that sometimes lead to conflict and resentment. First, the work lives of staff members are significantly different from those of faculty members. Staff members generally work on a fixed schedule. They do not come and go as they wish, but they watch faculty members doing so. They do not have long vacations from their regular duties. Most of them cannot work at home. They have more rules to follow than do faculty members. They do not have tenure and can often be fired at will. Many staff members are locals (this is especially important at SCUs that are in rural areas or small towns). Staff members do not see what faculty members are doing in the way of work when they are off campus. Many staff members are more student oriented and student centered than faculty members (and when they are not, that is a problem). In short, the work lives of most staff members are less autonomous, less flexible, and less cosmopolitan than the work lives of faculty members.

Wise faculty members learn that staff members can be enormously helpful or inflexibly obstructive. Wise faculty members nurture positive relationships with staff members in their own units, in the administrative units, at the registrar's office, at the book store, at the counseling center, and in traffic and security. They do not lord their autonomy, flexibility, expertise, or salary over the staff. Even less wise faculty members know how important the department administrative assistants are. If they learn to value other staff members in similar ways, life is easier for faculty members and their students.

Athletics

Perhaps in no other segment of American higher education is there more hypocrisy than in intercollegiate athletics. Just when observers are tempted to think that critics like Murray Sperber have gone over the top (Sperber, 2000), some individual athlete or coach, a university or the NCAA does something outrageous that makes the critics look good. Many fundamental values of academe get violated in big-time college sports. Yet in some ways athletics can be a constructive model for the rest of the campus. The simplistic idea that involvement in sports is character-building has long been discounted, but there are many positive things about involvement in intercollegiate sports (Toma, 2003). Coaches tend to work as hard as anyone on campus. Students work hard at their sports and often at their academic pursuits. Coaches are extremely positive about their institution when they are working there, perhaps to a fault. Coach-student interactions can be intense teaching-learning situations.

In other fundamental ways the collegial athletic and academic cultures are inconsistent. One outgrowth of this clash of cultures is that faculty members often find coaches to be aliens on the campus (and the feeling is largely mutual). This is particularly true of football coaches. A football coach who does not have some of the macho persona risks being criticized in the athletic subculture for being "too nice" to be an effective coach. The word "discipline" is a codeword in the athletic subculture. It stands for an approach to dealing with young people that reflects external control, an ill-defined form of "toughness," negativity, intimidation or fear, and related forms of authoritarian behavior.

A particular aspect of college sports that academics dislike is that so much goes on behind the scenes. There is nothing like due process involved in the hiring or firing of coaches. Personnel decisions cannot be discussed even though they cause 90% of the problems in the system. Of course, most faculty members do not really want the hassle of dealing with such things, but when things go wrong, it is those on the faculty who are there for the long term who have to deal with the fallout. Good administrators take measured responses. But because much of what goes on goes on in the dark when a coach is fired, there is no way of knowing if the athletic director's decision was decisive (and therefore good for the image à la editorial writers) or precipitous.

Another unfortunate aspect of the athletic culture is its emphasis on external control of student behavior. There is much paternalism in the way universities deal with athletes. Faculty members are often shocked by such treatment even in the small ways they see it in their courses or in the recruiting process or registration, class absences, and grading. If a psychologist were looking for attributions for athlete misbehavior, the focus would be on the extent to which external controls are applied to athletes—in their academic and athletic behavior. Psychologists tell us that when individuals are subjected to high degrees of external control, they may fail to fully develop internal controls.

Loyalty is a fragile thing in athletics too. Hardworking coaches can be fired for not winning. However, if they win too much, they may leave the university with little notice. The athletes so assiduously recruited to come and play for the coach are left behind (or have to give up a year of eligibility to transfer). Coaches are sensitive to status and, if they win, are more mobile than the best SCU faculty. Except in highly unusual situations, faculty members cannot sell good teaching—there is no market for good teaching. Based on faculty behavior in the flush job market of the 1960s, faculty members probably would not be any more loyal to their institutions than coaches under similar circumstances. Most faculty members are loyal first to their disciplines, not to their students or institutions. Salaries go with status. What has changed so much in recent years is the salary rate for what used to be considered "minor" sports. Swimming, baseball, and conditioning coaches at some major universities earn in the $150,000–$200,000 salary range (Eichelberger, 2005).

At most SCUs athletics do not have the prominence they have at many research universities. Many SCUs have maintained NCAA Division II status for football and other sports. However, there has been a trend over recent decades for more and more SCUs, especially those in the south, to drift toward NCAA

Division status with IAA status common for football. As we saw in Chapter 3, athletics is often used as a status generator. Many SCU athletic departments lust after "mid-major" status. Athletics can provide a positive part of the community culture for SCUs, but they must be kept under control.

Conclusion

There are many features of campus communities at the People's Universities that make them good places to be. This is especially true at SCUs in which there is a strong community of scholarship as well as a community of support, where students take learning seriously and where student learning is taken seriously. A mix of collegial and developmental cultures can foster the balanced academic life outlined in Chapter 5. In the next chapter, I raise some questions about the future of the community of scholarship at SCUs.

7 Threats and Opportunities at SCUs: A Murky Crystal Ball

In this final chapter I address what I see as trends that represent the greatest threats and opportunities to SCUs and their faculties and what we might do to respond to the threats and the opportunities. In doing so, I summarize and emphasize many of the arguments I made in the first six chapters.

The Big Threat and Its Consequences

There are educational, social, political, and economic trends that are likely to make it difficult to work in colleges and universities in the first half of the 21st century, especially in state-supported institutions (Altbach, 2005; Austin, 2002; Benjamin, 2003; Gregorian, 2005; O'Meara, Kaufman, & Kuntz, 2003; Ruben, 2004; Zemsky, Wegner, & Massy, 2005; Zusman, 2005). The greatest threat of all, a decline in funding, is occurring in many states where tax-based contributions to higher education have been declining and where higher education has been receiving a declining portion of overall state funds. Meanwhile in many states, particularly in the South and West, enrollment is increasing. The members of the large cohort of faculty members who were hired to teach the baby boomers are retiring. The consequence has been a cascading series of outcomes, one related to the next. The most important outcome of the falling state revenues combined with the need for new faculty members has been a startling increase in the number of part-time and full-time, nontenure-track faculty members hired to deal with growth and/or to replace faculty members who have left tenured or tenure-track positions (Leslie, 1999).

The presence of large numbers of part-time and nontenure-track faculty members on any one campus at any particular time is not in itself very threatening; however, the massive change to employing faculty members who only teach at an institution part-time and for a limited term can lead to a potentially devastating outcome. The traditional roles of the faculty member's job, teaching, research, and service, each based in the scholarly expertise of the faculty member, threaten to become unraveled or unbundled (Levine, 2000). The teaching of students, particularly undergraduates, could become piece work (Gregorian, 2005). Teachers might teach in campus classrooms but occupy no permanent office. They may teach courses for multiple unrelated institutions, live or online (Finkelstein, 2003). Research could become a commercialized, politicized function that may or may not be carried out on campuses by individuals who have little or no loyalty to a student body or a university. Certainly research will be done less frequently by faculty members who also teach undergraduates and serve their institutions and communities. The institutional and community service that is done could be offered by the shrinking portion of the faculty that works on one campus in what were once known as tenured or tenure-track positions.

Outside academia the unbundling of the teaching, research, and service functions of the faculty job might not appear to be problematic. Many critics of higher education have called for more emphasis on teaching (see Chapter 1). From their perspective, if faculty members were not under pressure to publish and conduct grant-funded research, perhaps teaching would be executed with greater quality and in greater quantity. Research might be more effectively conducted by those relatively few really bright individuals who could better carry out their cutting-edge research without the burdens of teaching. Less research might be done, but what would be lost would be an unproductive kind of research that never was published or was published in outlets no one ever reads. Service to the community might be more cheaply and efficiently carried out by agencies outside the university.

So what is the danger of unbundling the three roles of the faculty job? The glue that holds the three seemingly disparate functions is scholarship, particularly consumatory scholarship. The scholarship that holds the faculty roles together consists of the reading, thinking, creating, and talking with peers that does not necessarily lead to anything productive such as a journal article, a book, a musical score, or a work of art. In the knowledge society, what does not show up on a log of faculty activities or other accountings for faculty time is the actual acquisition and processing of knowledge. The great danger in unbundling teaching, research, and service is that no one has as part of the job that significant amount of time used by faculty members to become experts, to become scholars of their disciplines. It is that scholarly expertise that allows teaching, research, and service to be conducted with intellectual credibility. Young faculty members bring a fair amount of intellectual capital with them from graduate school. But all faculty members must continue to develop their scholarly expertise. Part-time faculty members and faculty members with heavy teaching loads eventually use up the intellectual capital they acquired in graduate school. If they are not given the time to continuously renew their knowledge and skills, high quality teaching and service cannot occur.

What in the short run looks like an efficient solution to staffing problems, hiring part-time and nontenure-track full-time faculty members, could ultimately end the community of scholarship that has made American higher education the envy of the world. At SCUs, the most significant damage would be done to teaching and learning. There will always be part-time faculty members, some of whom bring special skills that are greatly needed. However, SCUs should not use part-time faculty members to fill what have been tenure-track positions in healthy, growing departments. Using part-time faculty as a long-term solution to staffing problems can have severely negative consequences for fulfilling a university's mission. Loss of state funding causes many problems, but the unbundling of the expressions of scholarship and the subsequent undermining of scholarship itself would be the most damaging outcome.

Potential Opportunities for SCUs

In addition to the trend toward decreased public support there are several other trends that futurists consistently

see as influencing the future of higher education.
They include:

a) An increasingly diverse clientele

b) An increasing need for universities to provide expertise
   and applied research skills to help states and regions
   develop economically and culturally

c) Greater university involvement in public school
   reform, including the development of means for
   assessing student progress and the training and retention of qualified teachers

d) More emphasis on teaching innovations and
   effectiveness, especially in undergraduate education

e) Developing systems for delivering continuing education to adult students who need to retool or upgrade
   their skills

These trends will affect all of higher education.
However, what is most interesting about this list is that
the needs implied by each of these trends parallel what
historically have been strengths in the SCUs:

a) Access has been a hallmark in the development of the
   SCUs. Involvement with an increasingly diverse
   group of students will create problems, most dealing
   with questions of preparedness, but not different in
   kind from those problems SCUs have dealt with
   since the time of the normal schools. Increasing the
   historically poor graduation rates of the SCUs will be
   an essential goal.

b) While SCUs do not compare to research universities
   in the discovery of basic knowledge, SCUs and their
   predecessors have strong records of applying knowledge to practical cultural, social, political, and
   economic problems in their own regions (from the
   preparation of teachers to providing technical

expertise to industries and archeological or historical information for local museums).

c) SCUs have been specialists in working with public schools. Although the efforts of education schools have often been criticized, much of that criticism has been unfair and unwarranted (Labree, 2004). Education faculty members at SCUs have useful connections with the public schools, but it will be increasingly important for SCU faculty members outside the education schools to become involved in public schools.

d) SCUs have always been teaching institutions. Calls for more emphasis on teaching and the growing interest in the scholarship of teaching and learning play to a SCU strength. Moreover, it is clear that efforts at improving teaching already fit into the reward system at SCUs in ways that they do not at research universities (see Chapter 4).

e) The history of the SCUs has been one of taking courses and programs to people where the courses and programs are needed. Technological developments make this easier in many ways, but the basic attitudes and infrastructures for continuing education at SCUs precede technological developments.

Perhaps it is the SCU's time in higher education. The early history of higher education in America is a history of the development of the liberal arts college and the collegial culture (Geiger, 2005). The post–World War II period to the end of the 20th century was the era of the major research university with its emphasis on the generation of new knowledge. The liberal arts college has survived even in the era of the research university and will continue to serve an elite portion of the student population. More important, it will continue to provide an important standard for the liberal education of all students. The research university will continue to be a source, if not the major source, of new knowledge, particularly in the sciences, engineering, business, medicine, and law. However, if SCUs work on reputation rather than status and prestige, they may be the institutions that will be most needed in this century. There have been frequent calls for mission differentiation in the past (see Diamond, 1999; Zemsky et al., 2005) that may finally becoming a reality (Benjamin, 2003).

Threats to SCU Faculty Members

I believe there are at least two major threats to SCU faculty members' productivity. Both threats are attitudinal and both tend to influence faculty members in the sciences, social sciences, and humanities more than they do faculty members in more applied disciplines. The first threat is elitism. Elitism takes two forms among SCU faculty members. I discussed one, the desire for status and prestige, at length in Chapter 3. As I said there, it is very difficult for SCUs to attain high status within higher education and difficult for SCU faculty members to attain a high degree of status in their disciplines. A few individuals will succeed, but most who try are likely to be disappointed and unhappy about not being able to live up to unrealistic expectations. A significant source of unrealistic expectations at SCUs, especially expectations about publishing cutting-edge research findings, is the hearsay picked up from colleagues at meetings, parties, or in informal discussions on campus. Short of explicit written materials specifying research expectations, materials that are notoriously hard to obtain (Schoenfeld & Magnan, 1994), new faculty members should find out from library reference sources exactly how much research is actually being done on their campuses. At most SCUs the rhetorical publishing rate probably is higher than the real one (see Chapter 4).

The second form of elitism concerns attitudes about students. Because access has been such an important value of the SCUs and their predecessors, student bodies at SCUs are likely to include a substantial portion of students who are not well prepared for college (see Chapter 6). Too often faculty members call for more selective admissions standards or attribute their students' failures to learn to the students' lack of ability rather than to a lack of student effort or inadequate teaching. Equally damaging are those professors who respond to the perceived inadequacies of their students by failing to challenge them and institutions that reduce or degrade requirements (any introductory book on educational psychology makes clear that there is no substitute for time on task in the learning process). The democratic openness of the SCUs needs to be focused on admissions, not on the graduation of students who have not met high standards. Potential elitists should know that institutional selectivity (as indicated by SAT or ACT scores) does not predict instructional practices that encourage student engagement (Kuh & Pascarella, 2004). The degree to which an institution is selective is independent of the degree to which students at the institution are actively engaged in learning.

The second attitudinal threat to SCU faculty members is antivocationalism. All colleges and universities have moved toward more emphasis on preparing students for work (Grubb & Lazerson, 2005). Some faculty members are uncomfortable with this change. It is arguable how colleges and universities have really changed (Millard, 1991), but the perception that vocationalism has invaded the academy is real. Yet SCUs have historically targeted their programs to students who were much more likely to join the workforce after graduation than to attend graduate schools and become clones of their professors (see Chapter 2). During the transition from teachers colleges to state colleges, education programs were the target of antivocationalism. At many SCUs today the targets are likely to be health sciences, sport management, or criminal justice. There is simply no way to get around a strong orientation toward preparation for work at SCUs. It is in their history and their nature as institutions. Antivocationalists need to appreciate that many applied problems can and do require a degree of intellectual involvement equivalent to that involved in the classical liberal arts education (Millard, 1991; Schneider, 2005). At the same time, the champions of the traditional disciplines need to act as campus-wide citizens, ensuring that students in all programs are truly educated, not merely trained.

Faculty Opportunities

The current trends in higher education point to a special role for SCU faculty in focusing on teaching. At SCUs that are serving their missions, teaching will come first. What does it mean to say that teaching comes first? One clear meaning is that faculty members can spend more of their time on teaching functions than on anything else. It means teaching that is perceived to be effective will be supported and rewarded. It also means that teaching innovations, even risky ones that fail, will be considered worthwhile. It is becoming increasingly clear that student learning is a function of what the National Survey of Student Engagement has called *engagement* (see Chapters 5 and 6). At teaching institutions, students will be involved in a wide variety of learning activities. Finally, to say that teaching comes first is to say that teaching is a legitimate and valued source of scholarly activity. What is now called the scholarship of teaching and learning provides a mechanism for faculty members' involvement in their disciplines that mirrors traditional research and publication activities. Teaching innovations, demonstrations of student learning, and the assessment of teaching and learning will each count as professional development.

Some SCU administrators might say "but a faculty member has to do more than just teach." The inappropriateness of the "just" should be clear by now, but it is true that faculty members at almost every SCU will be expected to do more than teach. The traditional three-legged stool of teaching, research, and service continues to be used by all kinds of colleges and universities. At many SCUs traditional research and publication still carry the most weight in the evaluation of faculty members, which is a mistake (see Chapter 4). Some form of Boyer's (1990) expanded view of scholarship which I call "doing interesting things" sets better expectations for SCU faculty members. What are the interesting things that could and should be done and counted? Certainly, there always is room on the list for traditional basic research, especially if it involves students; however, large quantities of basic research should not be expected at SCUs. It is not normative (see Chapter 4), and only a tiny portion of the funds available to support research goes to institutions outside the top 100 major research universities (Benjamin, 2003). A broad area for doing interesting things is community service or engagement. Faculty members from many disciplines can provide scholarly expertise in consulting with agencies, businesses, and organizations on social, cultural, political, and economic issues. Most of this work is unlikely to lead to traditional forms of publication, but when done well, should be recognized and rewarded as scholarly activity. The same could be said about institutional service. Institutional service is given little or no weight in the evaluation of faculty members (e.g., Tierney & Benseman, 1996); however, when institutional service involves a genuine application of disciplinary expertise rather than carrying out simple chores, it too should be recognized and rewarded.

Surely there are many interesting things we have not yet seen or recognized. Our category of scholarly interesting things should be broad enough so that when new forms occur, they can be considered significant. Let me provide just one example of a needed interesting thing that is yet to appear. Colleges and universities have done a generally terrible job of educating their constituencies about what faculty members do. Legislators, parents, community members, and students all wonder how teaching in a classroom no more than 12 hours a week for 30 weeks a year can be considered a full-time job. Even staff members at our own institutions do not understand (Ruben, 2004). Those individuals who find ways to educate our constituencies effectively about the work of university professors need to be recognized and rewarded.

A Final Word

Faculty members who are willing to forego institutional and individual status and prestige may find the SCU the very best place to work. Despite the greediness of SCUs, they provide a wide array of professional opportunities for the well-rounded teacher-scholar. The hardest job for the productive SCU faculty member is finding a balance among the many interesting things there are to do. He or she should have little trouble with boredom.

Appendix: Self-Help for New Professors: A Sampler

There are dozens of books aimed at helping new faculty members get started on successful careers. I briefly annotate some of the more recent ones with a comment or two about their special relevance to the SCU professor. The books listed are very practical for the most part. Another genre of books tends to be more reflective, personal, and/or inspirational (e.g., Allitt, 2005; Palmer, 1998; Pickering, 2004; Roth, 1997; Tompkins, 1996).

General Advice on Academic Careers

Boice, R. (2000). *Advice for new faculty members: Nihil nimus.* Needham Heights, MA: Allyn & Bacon.

The author is a retired psychologist and faculty development administrator. He gives advice about teaching, research, and service. Boice recognizes that new faculty members often are so overwhelmed by all they need to do that they become paralyzed. He uses sets of rules in each domain to help the new faculty members see how everything can get done if you work at all of it in moderation (hence the Latin). Boice gets a little caught up in his own system, but there is a good deal of sound advice in all three areas. He gives no explicit recognition of the comprehensive university situation, but applying what he says would not involve a big stretch. The book includes a valuable set of annotated bibliographies for each domain.

DeNeef, A. L., & Goodwin, C. D. (Eds.). (1995). *The academic's handbook* (2nd ed.). Durham, NC: Duke University Press.

Most of the contributors to the expanded edition of this book (originally published in 1988) were or are at Duke University, thus the orientation here is from a distinctly research university perspective. Chapters include tips on finding a job, attaining tenure, obtaining grant funds for research, teaching techniques, doing research and publishing, and how to be political in the academy. There are also chapters on being a minority on campus, on academic freedom, and advising.

Ferris, S. P., Minielli, M. C., Phillips, K. R., & Mallard, J. S. (Eds.). (2003). *Beyond survival in the academy: A practical guide for beginning academics.* Cresskill, NJ: Hampton Press.

Of the books listed in this section, this one is most consistent with the SCU perspective. The authors, all former doctoral students in communications at Penn State have written a guide for new faculty that explicitly is not directed to those at research universities. It is modeled after an earlier book by some of these authors' teachers that was directed more at those who were (Phillips, Gouran, Kuehn, & Wood, 1994). The authors take the term *practical* in their title seriously. Their advice includes details such as the hidden costs of taking a new position such as parking fees, changing license plates in a new state, and joining a union. Ferris et al. are sensitive to the fact that the quality of one's teaching is likely to matter more outside the research sector. Again, the advice is highly specific, from developing a syllabus to learning to use the photocopier. The advice about research is also very practical with an emphasis on consulting with administrators on what will "count," and suggestions about alternative ways to publish. The chapters on service, networking, and preparing for tenure all give good nuts-and-bolts advice. Also included is a useful chapter titled "Developing the Whole Scholar," which summarizes the broader view of scholarship championed by Boyer (1990). Some new faculty members might feel that this book insults their intelligence, but I think it is much more likely that they will be delighted with the help.

Gibson, G. W. (1992). *Good start: A guidebook for new faculty in liberal arts colleges.* Bolton, MA: Anker.

Gibson's book is more philosophical than Ferris et al.'s and it is explicitly addressed to faculty members at liberal arts colleges. In an early footnote he points out the applicability of most of what he has to say to those at comprehensive universities, but the tone of most of the discussion is clearly directed to those working in the liberal arts tradition. Most helpful to SCU faculty is his broad view of scholarship. One important feature of that discussion is his emphasis on pacing the productive side of scholarship in a way that maintains a balance among different faculty activities. The book could use updating but still has much practical advice for faculty members at SCUs.

Lang, J. M. (2005). *Life on the tenure track: Lessons from the first year.* Baltimore, MD: The Johns Hopkins University Press.

Lang wrote a column for *The Chronicle of Higher Education* describing his experiences when he was looking for a job in academia. He continued writing for the *Chronicle* during his first year in a tenure-track position in English. This book is a retrospective expansion on his first year at a small New England college (Assumption College). This is not a how-to book, but much of Lang's experience will resonate with new faculty members at SCUs.

Lucas, C. J., & Murry, J. W., Jr. (2002). *New faculty: A practical guide for academic beginners.* New York, NY: Palgrave.

The title is accurate in including the term *practical*, yet there is a good deal of theory here. There is some psychology in the chapter on learning that I think is unsupportable (the section on individual differences stresses concepts of learning styles that do not have empirical support—see Chapter 6). Otherwise, this book is full of helpful information on teaching, getting published (with an emphasis on time management), getting grants, providing service, and legalities. The authors emphasize the need for new faculty members to learn how to say "no." The chapter on faculty service is introduced with a good discussion about how service needs to be shaped to the particular institutional type. Lucas and Murry point out that engagement in community service (applying expertise to community problems) has become increasingly important, especially at SCUs.

Menges, R. J., & Associates. (1999). *Faculty in new jobs: A guide to settling in, becoming established, and building institutional support.* San Francisco, CA: Jossey-Bass.

This is an edited volume that reports some data on studies of early faculty experience along with chapters giving advice about a range of issues, including stress, gender, color, mentoring, teaching, and learning.

Books on Teaching

Bain, K. (2004). *What the best college teachers do.* Cambridge, MA: Harvard University Press.

Bain's discussion of teaching springs from his systematic study of an unusual group of professors. They were professors who were identified by their students and others as having made a major difference in how their students thought, acted, and felt. They came from more than two dozen institutions and from many different disciplines. Bain observed them, live or on videotape, interviewed them, and looked at the materials they used in teaching. The chapters of the book are organized around questions about teaching. The questions focus on the teachers' knowledge of how students learn, their expectations for their students, how they plan, execute, and evaluate their teaching, and how they treat their students. Not all of what Bain has learned from these extraordinary teachers is readily applicable to the rest of us, but there is much here to aim for in trying to improve.

Brookfield, S. D., & Preskill, S. (2005). *Discussion as a way of teaching: Tools and techniques for democratic classrooms* (2nd ed.). San Francisco, CA: Jossey-Bass.

The authors provide a detailed nuts-and-bolts guide for using and maintaining discussions. They include chapters on preparing for discussion, asking good questions, and involving all students. They also give advice about how to start, maintain, and monitor online discussions.

Filene, P. (2005). *The joy of teaching: A practical guide for new college instructors.* Chapel Hill, NC: University of North Carolina Press.

In this very brief insider's view, Filene packs in lots of commonsense advice about lectures, discussions, grading, and relating to students. He recognizes that most professors do not work at major research universities and provides good examples that apply to all levels of higher education. A special contribution is a chapter titled "Teaching and Not Perishing," in which he provides wise advice about not spreading yourself too thin.

Fink, L. D. (2003). *Creating significant learning experiences: An integrated approach to designing college courses.* San Francisco, CA: Jossey-Bass.

Former director of the Instructional Development Program at the University of Oklahoma Dee Fink presents a comprehensive way of developing courses specifically designed to elicit higher-level thinking in students. He replaces Bloom's (1956) taxonomy with a taxonomy of six kinds of significant learning goals including foundational knowledge, application, integration, human dimension, caring, and learning how to learn. These goals can be achieved with a 3-phase, 12-step model of course design that involves planning, using learning activities in an organized instructional strategy, and evaluating students, the course, and the teaching. Fink's approach is ambitious. Adopting it is likely to require considerable time and effort and a concerted commitment to innovation. He tries hard to convince the reader that the effects on students make the work worthwhile.

Forsyth, D. R. (2003). *The professor's guide to teaching: Psychological principles and practices.* Washington, DC: American Psychological Association.

Forsyth is a psychologist and this book is strong in those areas you would expect a psychologist to know most about: testing, grading, course evaluation, and lecturing. Although aimed at all college teachers, this book has a strong social science air to it. More technical than most of the books in this genre, it is most likely to appeal to those with a data orientation. There is no explicit recognition of the special circumstances of the comprehensive university faculty member.

Lowman, J. (1995). *Mastering the techniques of teaching* (2nd ed.). San Francisco, CA: Jossey-Bass.

The first edition of this book was published in 1984, making it one of the classics of the genre. Lowman professes to be taking a conservative stance on teaching, meaning that his aim is to help college professors improve their traditional teaching. Lowman is an expert on teaching large classes at a research university and much of his book is aimed at improving teaching in the traditional lecture-discussion format. Although many more recent books give a broader perspective, this book provides many helpful suggestions for teachers who spend a lot of time in the traditional college lecture hall.

McKeachie, W. J. (2002). *McKeachie's teaching tips: Strategies, research, and theory for college and university teachers* (11th ed.). Boston, MA: Houghton Mifflin.

Depending on which one of the editions of McKeachie's book you happen to pick up (the 12th is due out in 2006), you will get a somewhat different mix of chapter topics. All the editions include a basic set of recommendations on dozens of topics, including how to lecture, direct discussions, run laboratories, use simulations, make exams, and use visual aids. There are also chapters on ethics, student motivation, course evaluation, and dealing with large classes, some of which have been authored by others besides McKeachie. Several generations of beginning college teachers at all levels have received copies of *Teaching Tips* from the deans or department heads who hired them.

Nilson, L. B. (2003). *Teaching at its best: A research-based resource for college instructors* (2nd ed.). Bolton, MA: Anker.

Nilson's book is a very practical and well-conceptualized resource for teaching. It provides advice from the design of the course objectives and the syllabus to what to do on the first day of class and in office hours. It also provides guidance on many different teaching techniques and on the assessment of students and course evaluation. It is especially helpful to new faculty members, yet even experienced faculty members would find much useful information here.

Svinicki, M. D. (Ed.). (2000). *New directions for teaching and learning: No. 80. Teaching and learning on the edge of the millennium: Building on what we have learned.* San Francisco, CA: Jossey-Bass.

This edited volume of contributions in honor of the 20th year of the *New Directions for Teaching and Learning* series was designed as an update of the literature on teaching and learning. The authors of the chapters had edited issues in the series. Their brief summaries of literature on learning, teaching, group learning, technology, teaching for critical thinking and other issues provide succinct outlines of the relevant resources for someone who wants to explore the issues further. Although none of the topics covered are specifically directed at comprehensive university faculty members, Chickering and Gamson's chapter on the seven principles of good practice in undergraduate education might be of special interest.

Weimer, M. (1996). *Survival skills for scholars: Vol. 7. Improving your classroom teaching.* Thousand Oaks, CA: Sage.

This is volume 7 of 19 volumes in Sage's *Survival Skills for Scholars* series (other volumes include a focus on getting a job, getting published, earning tenure, obtaining consulting work, planning conferences, serving on committees, and chairing departments). It covers much of the same territory as the Nilson (2003) book but in much less detail.

Special Topics

Caplan, P. J. (1993). *Lifting a ton of feathers: A woman's guide to surviving in the academic world.* Toronto, Canada: University of Toronto Press.

I hope this book is dated because it contains many very scary stories about discrimination against women in academe. Unfortunately, too much of what Caplan says here still applies in some situations. She goes into great detail about specific instances of sexism but also provides many practical suggestions about how to deal with discriminatory behavior. She does not say much about "less prestigious" settings except to indicate that there are more women there. The truth of the myths Caplan discusses can be debated at all types of universities (her myths include that academia is a pure meritocracy, that only objective standards are used in tenure and promotion decisions, that universities are liberal, open places, and that all scholarly work is of equal value).

Diamond, R. M. (2004). *Preparing for promotion, tenure, and annual review: A faculty guide* (2nd ed.). Bolton, MA: Anker.

Diamond's very practical book has two parts. In Part I he gives detailed advice on what and who faculty members should know in the evaluation process, what should be collected to document their work, and how to present a complete picture in preparation for review. Part II provides simple instruments for collecting data on teaching, collegiality, and service and examples of how to document the scholarly contribution of various products (e.g., textbooks, curricula, student plays, new courses, museum exhibits, and software). Of special interest to those at comprehensive universities, Diamond discusses how to tie faculty efforts to institutional mission and vision statements.

Finkel, D. L. (2000). *Teaching with your mouth shut.* Portsmouth, NH: Boynton/Cook.

Finkel argues for student-centered approaches to teaching, including book discussions, inquiry learning, writing, and team teaching. Teachers at all kinds of institutions and across disciplines will find many good ideas here.

Frost, P. J., & Taylor, M. S. (1996). *Rhythms of academic life: Personal accounts of careers in academia.* Thousand Oaks, CA: Sage.

In this volume, professors, almost all from business schools, give autobiographical accounts. Some of the accounts focus on overall career paths while others focus more specifically on experiences in teaching, journal reviewing and editing, research, consulting, and many other academic tasks. Almost all the contributors are from research universities and only a few provide advice that would particularly fit the SCU faculty role, but much of what they say can be extrapolated across institutions and disciplines.

Grunert, J. (1997). *The course syllabus: A learning-centered approach.* Bolton, MA: Anker.

Grunert argues that a syllabus should be a tool for student learning and an indication of the instructor's scholarship. She outlines her rationale and discusses the many functions of a good syllabus. A good portion of the book consists of concrete examples of the contents of different portions of a syllabus. The annotated suggested readings provide background for the different portions of the learning-oriented syllabus.

Lee, V. S. (Ed.). (2004). *Teaching and learning through inquiry: A guidebook for institutions and instructors.* Sterling, VA: Stylus.

All the contributors to this edited volume focus on the inquiry method of teaching; however, they represent a very wide range of disciplines, from psychology and languages to engineering and food science. Once again, there is nothing particularly directed to the SCU environment here, but the inquiry method certainly can be and is used in the SCU setting.

McManus, D. A. (2005). *Leaving the lectern: Cooperative learning and the critical first days of students working in groups.* Bolton, MA: Anker.

This is a very personal journal of how an oceanography professor at a research university gave up lecturing and adopted the use of cooperative projects in an upper-level course. McManus documents what he did before the change, his tentative first steps in making what was a radical change for him, the problems he encountered, and the joy he experienced in seeing students learning in new ways. He also describes his search for connections to others on and off his campus who share his interest in teaching innovations. The result is a model for all those who need a confidence boost for making changes in their teaching.

Seldin, P. (2004). *The teaching portfolio: A practical guide to improved performance and promotion/tenure decisions* (3rd ed.). Bolton, MA: Anker.

The teaching portfolio has become an increasingly popular mechanism for faculty members to document their teaching methods, philosophy, and outcomes. Peter Seldin is one of the strongest proponents of the use of portfolios in higher education. In this edition Seldin provides a brief introduction to the concept of the teaching portfolio. Other contributors then provide discussions of electronic forms of portfolios and how to update them. The bulk of the book, however, is a collection of chapters on how portfolios are used at many different types of institutions and 22 examples of portfolios from teachers from a wide variety of disciplines.

Stanley, C. A., & Porter, M. E. (Eds.). (2002). *Engaging large classes: Strategies and techniques for college faculty.* Bolton, MA: Anker.

For someone who has never experienced very large classes (as a student or as an instructor)—classes of 70, 80, or 700—reading the selections in this book is like reading a travelogue of a trip to an exotic foreign land. For those who regularly deal with very large classes, this book offers many realistic ideas for increasing the likelihood students will perceive that they have had a meaningful learning experience. As might be expected, most of the contributors to this volume teach at large research universities, although a couple of state comprehensive universities are represented. The first part of the book consists of advice given by the veterans of the mega-classes ranges from promoting civility, getting students actively involved, using graduate and undergraduate teaching assistants, and using technology. The second part provides examples of teachers' experiences in large classes in a wide variety of disciplines. A particularly useful chapter in the second part is the editors' summary of key concepts.

Zubizarreta, J. (2004). *The learning portfolio: Reflective practice for improving student learning.* Bolton, MA: Anker.

Zubizarreta's book is a complement to Seldin's (2004) in which he shows how portfolios can be used with students. The first part of the book is a primer on the use of portfolios, including details on how to create and use student learning portfolios. The second part of the book provides descriptions of models of the use of portfolios by faculty members at all kinds of colleges and universities in many different disciplines. The contributors highlight the central role of metacognitive reflection in learning portfolios. The last part of the book includes examples of student portfolios and illustrative instructional materials such as assessment tools, assignments, and exercises related to student portfolios.

Academic Novels

It is arguable how helpful reading novels set in academia might be to new faculty members. Some novels about professors may provide insights into the inner workings of colleges and universities that could forewarn the new faculty member about the political and social pitfalls on campus. Many could provide comic relief. Some of the same ones could convince a new recruit of the folly of entering the profession. Kramer's *The American College*

Novel (2003) is a comprehensive annotated bibliography that is a guide to hundreds of novels. Most academic novels are set at small colleges or large research universities. A few take place on SCU–like campuses. Perhaps the best of these is Richard Russo's *Straight Man* (Vintage Books, 1997).

Bibliography

Adams, K. A. (2002). *What colleges and universities want in new faculty*. Washington, DC: Association of American Colleges and Universities.

Aitkin, D. (1991). How research came to dominate higher education and what ought to be done about it. *Oxford Review of Education, 17*(3), 235–247.

Allitt, P. (2005). *I'm the teacher, you're the student: A semester in the university classroom*. Philadelphia, PA: University of Pennsylvania Press.

Alpert, D. (1985). Performance and paralysis: The organizational context of the American research university. *Journal of Higher Education, 56*(3), 241–281.

Altbach, P. G. (1995). Problems and possibilities: The U.S. academic profession. *Studies in Higher Education, 20*(1), 27–44.

Altbach, P. G. (2005). Harsh realities: The professoriate faces a new century. In P. G. Altbach, R. O. Berdahl, & P. J. Gumport (Eds.), *American higher education in the twenty-first century: Social, political, and economic challenges* (2nd ed., pp. 287–314). Baltimore, MD: The Johns Hopkins University Press.

Altenbaugh, R. J., & Underwood, K. (1990). The evolution of normal schools. In J. I. Goodlad, R. Soder, & K. A. Sirotnik (Eds.), *Places where teachers are taught* (pp. 136–186). San Francisco, CA: Jossey-Bass.

American Association of State Colleges and Universities. (1999). *Facing change: Building the faculty of the future*. Washington, DC: Author.

American Association of State Colleges and Universities. (2002). *Findings and trends: Fall 1990–Fall 2000: AASCU/NASULGC Enrollment Report*. Retrieved March 27, 2006, from http://www.aascu.org/pdf/02_enrollment.pdf

American Association of University Professors. (2001). *Policy documents and reports* (9th ed.). Washington, DC: Author.

Anderson, M. (1992). *Impostors in the temple: The decline of the American University*. New York, NY: Simon & Schuster.

Aronson, J., Fried, C. B., & Good, C. (2002). Reducing the effects of stereotype threat on African-American college students by shaping theories of intelligence. *Journal of Experimental Social Psychology, 38*(2), 113–125.

Astin, A. W. (1984). Student involvement: A developmental theory for higher education. *Journal of College Student Personnel, 25*(4), 297–308.

Astin, A. W. (1985). *Achieving educational excellence.* San Francisco, CA: Jossey-Bass.

Astin, A. W. (1996). Involvement in learning revisited: Lessons we have learned. *Journal of College Student Development, 37*(2), 123–134.

Astin, A. W., & Chang, M. J. (1995). Colleges that emphasize research and teaching: Can you have your cake and eat it too? *Change, 27*(5), 45–49.

Atkinson, M. P. (2001). The scholarship of teaching and learning: Reconceptualizing scholarship and transforming the academy. *Social Forces, 79*(4), 1217–1229.

Austin, A. E. (2002). Creating a bridge to the future: Preparing new faculty to face changing expectations in a shifting context. *Review of Higher Education, 26*(2), 119–144.

Badley, G. (2003). Improving the scholarship of teaching and learning. *Innovations in Education and Teaching International, 40*(3), 303–309.

Baldridge, J. V., Curtis, D. V., Ecker, G., & Riley, G. L. (1978). *Policy making and effective leadership: A national study of academic management.* San Francisco, CA: Jossey-Bass.

Baldwin, R. G., Lunceford, C. J., & Vanderlinden, K. E. (2005). Faculty in the middle years: Illuminating an overlooked phase of academic life. *Review of Higher Education, 29*(1), 97–118.

Bardo, J. W. (Ed.). (1990). *Defining the missions of AASCU institutions.* Washington, DC: American Association of State Colleges and Universities.

Barzun, J. (1991). *Begin here: The forgotten conditions of teaching and learning* (M. Philipson, Ed.). Chicago, IL: University of Chicago Press.

Becher, T. (1989). *Academic tribes and territories: Intellectual enquiry and the cultures of disciplines.* Milton Keynes, England: The Society for Research into Higher Education/ Open University Press.

Bender, E. T. (2005). CASTLs in the air: The SOTL "movement" in mid-flight. *Change, 37*(5), 40–49.

Benjamin, R. (2003). The environment of American higher education: A constellation of changes. *The Annals of the American Academy of Political and Social Science, 585*(1), 8–30.

Bergquist, W. H. (1992). *The four cultures of the academy: Insights and strategies for improving leadership in collegiate organizations.* San Francisco, CA: Jossey-Bass.

Birnbaum, R. (1988). *How colleges work: The cybernetics of academic organization and leadership.* San Francisco, CA: Jossey-Bass.

Bisk, R. (2000, December 15). The new face of state colleges [Letter to the editor]. *The Chronicle of Higher Education,* p. B20

Blackburn, R. T., & Lawrence, J. H. (1995). *Faculty at work: Motivation, expectation, satisfaction.* Baltimore, MD: The Johns Hopkins University Press.

Bloom, B. S. (Ed.). (1956). *Taxonomy of eductional objectives: Handbook I. Cognitive domain.* White Plains, NY: Longman.

Bogue, E. G., & Aper, J. (2000). *Exploring the heritage of American higher education: The evolution of philosophy and policy.* Phoenix, AZ: American Council on Higher Education/Oryx Press.

Bowen, H. R., & Schuster, J. H. (1986). *American professors: A national resource imperiled.* New York, NY: Oxford University Press.

Boyer, E. L. (1990). *Scholarship reconsidered: Priorities of the professoriate.* Princeton, NJ: The Carnegie Foundation for the Advancement of Teaching.

Bransford, J. D., Brown, A. L., & Cocking, R. R. (1999). *How people learn: Brain, mind, experience, and school.* Washington, DC: National Academy Press.

Braxton, J. M. (Ed.). (1996). *New Directions for Institutional Research: No. 90. Faculty teaching and research: Is there a conflict?* San Francisco, CA: Jossey-Bass.

Braxton, J. M., & Bayer, A. E. (1986). Assessing faculty scholarly performance. In J. W. Cresswell (Ed.), *New Directions for Institutional Research: No. 50. Measuring faculty research performance* (pp. 25–42). San Francisco, CA: Jossey-Bass.

Braxton, J. M., & Del Favero, M. (2002). Evaluating scholarship performance: Traditional and emergent assessment templates. In C. L. Colbeck (Ed.) *New Directions for Institutional Research: No. 114. Evaluating faculty performance* (pp. 19–32). San Francisco, CA: Jossey-Bass.

Brewer, D. J., Gates, S. M., & Goldman, C. A. (2002). *In pursuit of prestige: Strategy and competition in U.S. higher education.* New Brunswick, NJ: Transaction.

Brint, S., Riddle, M., Turk-Bicakci, L., & Levy, C. S. (2005). From the liberal to the practical arts in American colleges and universities: Organizational analysis and curricular change. *The Journal of Higher Education, 76*(2), 151–180.

Brookfield, S. D., & Preskill, S. (1999). *Discussion as a way of teaching: Tools and techniques for democratic classrooms.* San Francisco, CA: Jossey-Bass.

Burke, D. L. (1988). *A new academic marketplace.* Westport, CT: Greenwood.

Caesar, T. (1991). On teaching at a second-rate university. *South Atlantic Quarterly, 90*(3), 449–467.

Caesar, T. (2000). *Traveling through the boondocks: In and out of academic hierarchy.* Albany, NY: State University of New York Press.

Caplow, T., & McGee, R. J. (1958). *The academic marketplace.* New York, NY: Basic Books.

Clark, B. R. (1987). *The academic life: Small worlds, different worlds.* Princeton, NJ: The Carnegie Foundation for the Advancement of Teaching.

Cochran, L. H. (1992). *Publish or perish: The wrong issue.* Cape Girardeau, MO: Step Up.

Coser, L. (1974). *Greedy institutions: Patterns of undivided commitment.* New York, NY: The Free Press.

Creamer, E. G. (1998). *Assessing faculty publication productivity: Issues of equity.* (ASHE-ERIC Higher Education Report, Vol. 26, No. 2). Washington, DC: George Washington University Graduate School of Education and Human Development. (ERIC Document Reproduction Service No. ED420242)

Cuban, L. (1999). *How scholars trumped teachers: Change without reform in university curriculum, teaching, and research 1890–1990.* New York, NY: Teachers College Press.

Daly, W. T. (1994). Teaching and scholarship: Adapting American higher education to hard times. *Journal of Higher Education, 65*(1), 45–57.

Damrosch, D. (1995). *We scholars: Changing the culture of the university.* Cambridge, MA: Harvard University Press.

Dey, E. L., Milem, J. F., & Berger, J. B. (1997). Changing patterns of publication productivity: Accumulative advantage or institutional isomorphism? *Sociology of Education, 70*(4), 308–323.

Diamond, R. M. (1999). *Aligning faculty rewards with institutional mission: Statements, policies, and guidelines.* Bolton, MA: Anker.

Dinham, S. M. (1999). New faculty talk about stress. In R. J. Menges & Associates (Eds.), *Faculty in new jobs: A guide to settling in, becoming established, and building institutional support* (pp. 39–58). San Francisco, CA: Jossey-Bass.

Domingo, V. (2000, December 15). The new face of state colleges [Letter to the editor]. *The Chronicle of Higher Education*, p. B20

Douglas, G. H. (1992). *Education without impact: How our universities fail the young.* New York, NY: Carol.

Dunham, E. A. (1969). *Colleges of the forgotten Americans: A profile of state colleges and regional universities.* New York, NY: McGraw-Hill.

Dunn, R., & Griggs, S. A. (2000). *Practical approaches to using learning styles in higher education.* Westport, CT: Bergin & Garvey.

Dweck, C. S. (2000). *Self-theories: Their role in motivation, personality, and development.* Philadelphia, PA: Psychology Press.

Eble, K. E. (1962). *The profane comedy: American higher education in the sixties.* New York, NY: Macmillan.

Ehrenberg, R. G. (2002). Reaching for the brass ring: The "U. S. News & World Report"rankings and competition. *Review of Higher Education, 26*(2), 145–162.

Eichelberger, C. (2005). *Coaches' pay surge roils colleges: $230,000 to train runners.* Retrieved April 18, 2006, from: http://quote.bloomberg.com/apps/news?pid=nifea&&sid=a C2XHZdyzqN8

Eisenmann, L. (1990). The influence of bureaucracy and markets: Teacher education in Pennsylvania. In J. I. Goodlad, R. Soder, & K. A. Sirotnik (Eds.), *Places where teachers are taught* (pp. 287–329). San Francisco, CA: Jossey-Bass.

Elsbree, W. S. (1939). *The American teacher: Evolution of a profession in a democracy.* New York, NY: American Book Company.

Evenden, E. S. (1938). Graduate work in teachers colleges. *17th Yearbook of the American Association of Teachers Colleges,* 122–133.

Fairweather, J. S. (1996). *Faculty work and public trust: Restoring the value of teaching and public service in American academic life.* Needham Heights, MA: Allyn & Bacon.

Fairweather, J. S. (2002). The mythologies of faculty productivity: Implications for institutional policy and decision making. *Journal of Higher Education, 73*(1), 26–48.

Feldman, K. A. (1987). Research productivity and scholarly accomplishment of college teachers as related to their instructional effectiveness: A review and exploration. *Research in Higher Education, 26*(3), 227–298.

Fink, L. D. (2003). *Creating significant learning experiences: An integrated approach to designing college courses.* San Francisco, CA: Jossey-Bass.

Finkelstein, M. (2003). The morphing of the American academic profession. *Liberal Education, 89*(4), 6–15.

Finnegan, D. E. (1991). *Opportunity knocked: The origins of contemporary comprehensive colleges and universities* (Working Paper No. 6). Boston, MA: New England Resource Center for Higher Education.

Finnegan, D. E. (1993a). Segmentation in the academic labor market: Hiring cohorts in comprehensive universities. *Journal of Higher Education, 64*(6), 621–656.

Finnegan, D. E. (1993b, April). *Departmental ethos and faculty satisfaction: A case study from two comprehensive universities.* Paper presented at the annual meeting of the American Educational Research Association, Atlanta, GA.

Finnegan, D. E. (1994, April). *Heads and tails: Burton Clark's The academic life and the limits of metaphor.* Paper presented at the annual meeting of the American Educational Research Association, New Orleans, LA.

Finnegan, D. E. (1997). The academic marketplace and the motivation to teach. In J. L. Bess (Ed.), *Teaching well and liking it: Motivating faculty to teach effectively* (pp. 337–361). Baltimore, MD: The Johns Hopkins University Press.

Fogg, P. (2004, April 16). For these professors, "practice" is perfect. *The Chronicle of Higher Education*, pp. A12–A14.

Fox, M. F. (1985). Publication, performance, and reward in science and scholarship. In J. C. Smart (Ed.), *Higher education: Handbook of theory and research* (Vol. 1, pp. 255–282). New York, NY: Agathon Press.

Fulton, O., & Trow, M. (1974). Research activity in higher education. *Sociology of Education, 47*(1), 29–73.

Gamson, Z. F. (1997, Summer). The stratification of the academy. *Social Text, 51*, 67–73.

Gaston, J. (1978). *The reward system in British and American science.* New York, NY: Wiley.

Geiger, R. L. (2005). The ten generations of American higher education. In P. G. Altbach, R. O. Berdahl, & P. J. Gumport (Eds.), *American higher education in the twenty-first century: Social, political, and economic challenges* (2nd ed., pp. 38–70). Baltimore, MD: The Johns Hopkins University Press.

Giroux, H. A. (1999). *Corporate culture and the attack on higher education and public schooling.* Bloomington, IN: Phi Delta Kappa Educational Foundation.

Gittenstein, R. B. (2000, December 15). The new face of state colleges [Letter to the editor]. *The Chronicle of Higher Education*, p. B20.

Glassick, C. E., Huber, M. T., & Maeroff, G. I. (1997). *Scholarship assessed: Evaluation of the professoriate.* San Francisco, CA: Jossey-Bass.

Glazer, J. S. (1993). The doctor of arts: Retrospect and prospect. In L. Richlin (Ed.), *New directions for teaching and learning: No. 54: Preparing faculty for new conceptions of scholarship* (pp. 15–25). San Francisco, CA: Jossey-Bass.

Glover, J. A. (2001). Scholarly publications: It's still publish or perish. In K. D. Hostetler, R. M. Sawyer, & K. W. Prichard (Eds.), *The art and politics of college teaching: A practical guide for the beginning professor* (2nd ed., pp. 217–226). New York, NY: Peter Lang.

Goodlad, J. I. (1990). Connecting the present to the past. In J. I. Goodlad, R. Soder, & K. A. Sirotnik (Eds.), *Places where teachers are taught* (pp. 3–39). San Francisco, CA: Jossey-Bass.

Gow, L., & Kember, D. (1990). Does higher education promote independent learning? *Higher Education, 19*(3), 307–322.

Gregorian, V. (2005). Six challenges to the American university. In R. H. Hersh, & J. Merrow (Eds.), *Declining by degrees: Higher education at risk* (pp. 77–96). New York, NY: Palgrave Macmillan.

Grubb, W. N., & Lazerson, M. (2005). Vocationalism in higher education: The triumph of the education gospel. *Journal of Higher Education, 76*(1), 1–25.

Hall, D. E. (2002). *The academic self: An owner's manual.* Columbus, OH: Ohio State Press.

Harcleroad, F. F., Sagen, H. B., & Molen, C. T., Jr. (1969). *The developing state colleges and universities: Historical background, current status, and future plans.* Iowa City, IA: The American College Testing Program.

Harper, C. A. (1935). *Development of the teachers college in the United States.* Bloomington, IL: McKnight and McKnight.

Henderson, B. B., & Buchanan, H. E. (2006a). *Publish or perish at comprehensive universities: Rhetoric or reality?* Manuscript in preparation.

Henderson, B. B., & Buchanan, H. E. (2006b). *The scholarship of teaching and learning: A special niche for faculty at comprehensive universities?* Manuscript submitted for publication.

Henderson, B. B., & Kane, W. D. (1991). Caught in the middle: Faculty and institutional status and quality in state comprehensive universities. *Higher Education, 22*(4), 339–350.

Herbst, J. (1989). Teacher preparation in the nineteenth century: Institutions and purposes. In D. Warren (Ed.), *American teachers: Histories of a profession at work* (pp. 213–236). New York, NY: Macmillan.

Hersh, R. H., & Merrow, J. (Eds.). (2005). *Declining by degrees: Higher education at risk.* New York, NY: Palgrave Macmillan.

Holland, E. O. (1912/1972). *The Pennsylvania state normal school and public school system.* New York, NY: AMS Press.

Huber, M. T. (2001). Balancing acts: Designing careers around the scholarship of teaching. *Change, 33*(4), 21–30.

Hutchings, P., & Shulman, L. S. (1999). The scholarship of teaching: New elaborations, new developments. *Change, 31*(6), 10–15.

Jackameit, W. P. (1973). *The political, social, and economic factors in the shaping of the structure of public higher education in West Virginia: A history, 1863–1969.* Ed.D. dissertation, College of William and Mary.

James, W. (1890). *The principles of psychology* (Vols. 1–2). New York, NY: Henry Holt & Co.

James, W. (1903, March). The Ph.D. octopus. *Harvard Monthly, 36*(1), 1–9.

Jenkins, A., Breen, R., Lindsay, R., & Brew, A. (2003). *Reshaping teaching in higher education: Linking teaching with research.* London, England: Kogan Page.

Johnson, W. R. (1989). Teachers and teacher training in the twentieth century. In D. Warren (Ed.), *American teachers: Histories of a profession at work* (pp. 237–256). New York, NY: Macmillan.

Johnston, R. (1998). The university of the future: Boyer revisited. *Higher Education, 36*(3), 253–272.

Kent, R. A. (Ed.). (1930). *Higher education in America.* Boston, MA: Ginn & Co.

Kramer, J. E., Jr. (2003). *The American college novel: An annotated bibliography* (2nd ed.). Lanham, MD: Scarecrow Press.

Kuh, G. D. (2003). What we're learning about student engagement from NSSE: Benchmarks for effective educational practices. *Change, 35*(2), 24–32.

Kuh, G. D., Gonyea, R. M., & Williams, J. M. (2005). What students expect from college and what they get. In T. E. Miller, B. E. Bender, J. H. Schuh, & Associates, *Promoting reasonable expectations: Aligning student and institutional views of the college experience* (pp. 34–64). San Francisco, CA: Jossey-Bass.

Kuh, G. D., & Pascarella, E. T. (2004). What does institutional selectivity tell us about educational quality? *Change, 36*(5), 52–58.

Labaree, D. F. (1997). *How to succeed in school without really learning: The credentials race in American education.* New Haven, CT: Yale University Press.

Labaree, D. F. (2004). *The trouble with ed schools.* New Haven, CT: Yale University Press.

Lambert, N. M., & McCombs, B. L. (Eds.). (1997). *How students learn: Reforming schools through learner-centered education.* Washington, DC: American Psychological Association.

Learned, W. S., & Wood, B. D. (1938). *The student and his knowledge: A report to the Carnegie Foundation on the results of the high school and college examinations of 1928, 1930, and 1932* (Bulletin No. 29). New York, NY: The Carnegie Foundation for the Advancement of Teaching.

Leatherman, C. (1990, December 5). Definition of faculty scholarship must be expanded to include teaching, Carnegie Foundation says. *The Chronicle of Higher Education,* pp. A1, A16–A17.

Lee, V. S. (Ed.). (2004). *Teaching and learning through inquiry: A guidebook for institutions and instructors.* Sterling, VA: Stylus.

Leloudis, J. L. (1996). *Schooling the New South: Pedagogy, self, and society in North Carolina, 1880–1920.* Chapel Hill, NC: University of North Carolina Press.

Leslie, D. W. (Ed.). (1999). *New Directions for Higher Education: No. 104. The growing use of part-time faculty: Understanding causes and effects.* San Francisco, CA: Jossey-Bass.

Leslie, D. W. (2002). Resolving the dispute: Teaching is academe's core value. *Journal of Higher Education, 73*(1), 49–73.

Levine, A. E. (2000, October 27). The future of colleges: 9 inevitable changes. *The Chronicle of Higher Education,* p. B10.

Lewis, L. S. (1975/1998). *Scaling the ivory tower: Merit and its limits in academic careers* (2nd ed.). New Brunswick, NJ: Transaction.

Lewis, M. (1997). *Poisoning the ivy: The seven deadly sins and other vices of higher education in America.* Armonk, NY: M. E. Sharpe.

Light, D. W., Jr. (1974). Introduction: The structure of the academic professions. *Sociology of Education, 47*(1), 2–28.

Lovett, C. M. (2005, January 21). The perils of pursuing prestige. *The Chronicle of Higher Education,* p. B20.

Lucas, C. J., & Murry, J. W., Jr. (2002). *New faculty: A practical guide for academic beginners.* New York, NY: Palgrave.

Lynton, E. A. (1983). A crisis of purpose: Reexamining the role of the university. *Change, 15*(6), 18–23, 53.

Mandell, R. D. (1977). *The professor game.* Garden City, NY: Doubleday.

Massy, W. F., & Zemsky, R. (1994). Faculty discretionary time: Departments and the "academic ratchet." *Journal of Higher Education, 65*(1), 1–22.

McCormick, A. C., & Zhao, C. M. (2005). Rethinking and reframing the Carnegie Classification. *Change, 37*(5), 50–57.

McKeachie, W. J. (1994). *Teaching tips: Strategies, research, and theory for college and university teachers* (9th ed.). Lexington, MA: D. C. Heath.

McMillin, L. A., & Berberet, W. G. (Eds.). (2002). *A new academic compact: Revisioning the relationship between faculty and their institutions.* Bolton, MA: Anker.

Menges, R. J., & Associates. (1999). *Faculty in new jobs: A guide to settling in, becoming established, and building institutional support.* San Francisco, CA: Jossey-Bass.

Merton, R. K. (1968). The Matthew Effect in science: The reward and communications systems of science are considered. *Science, 159*(3810), 56–63.

Millard, R. M. (1991). *Today's myths and tomorrow's realities: Overcoming obstacles to academic leadership in the 21st century.* San Francisco, CA: Jossey-Bass.

Mirochnik, E., & Sherman, D. C. (Eds.). (2002). *Passion and pedagogy: Relation, creation, and transformation in teaching.* New York, NY: Peter Lang.

Morphew, C. C. (2002). A rose by any other name: Why colleges become universities. *Review of Higher Education, 25*(2), 207–223.

Morphew, C. C., Toma, J. D., & Hedstrom, C. Z. (2001, November). *The public liberal arts college: Case studies of institutions that have bucked the trend toward "upward drift". . . and the implications for mission and market.* Paper presented at the meeting of the Association for the Study of Higher Education, Richmond, VA.

National Survey of Student Engagement. (2004). *2004 annual survey results.* Retrieved March 27, 2006, from: http://nsse.iub.edu/ 2004_annual_report/pdf/annual_report.pdf

Nerad, M., & Cerny, J. (1999). From rumors to facts: Career outcomes of English Ph.D.s: Results from the Ph.D.'s–Ten years later study. *Communicator, 32*(7), 1–12.

Ogren, C. A. (1995). Where coeds were coeducated: Normal schools in Wisconsin, 1870–1920. *History of Education Quarterly, 35*(1), 1–26.

Ogren, C. A. (2003). Rethinking the "nontraditional" student from a historical perspective: State normal schools in the late nineteenth and early twentieth centuries. *Journal of Higher Education, 74*(6), 640–664.

Ogren, C. A. (2005). *The American state normal school: "An instrument of great good."* New York, NY: Palgrave Macmillan.

O'Meara, K. A. (2005). Encouraging multiple forms of scholarship in faculty reward systems: Does it make a difference? *Research in Higher Education, 46*(5), 479–510.

O'Meara, K. A., Kaufman, R. R., & Kuntz, A. M. (2003). Faculty work in difficult times. *Liberal Education, 89*(4), 16–23.

Osborn, J. J., Jr. (1971). *Paper chase.* Boston, MA: Houghton Mifflin.

Pace, C. R., & Connolly, M. (2000). Where are the liberal arts? *Research in Higher Education, 41*(1), 53–65.

Park, S. M. (1996). Research, teaching, and service: Why shouldn't women's work count? *Journal of Higher Education, 67*(1), 46–84.

Palmer, P. J. (1998). *The courage to teach: Exploring the inner landscape of a teacher's life.* San Francisco, CA: Jossey-Bass.

Pangburn, J. M. (1932). *The evolution of the teachers college.* New York, NY: Teachers College Columbia University.

Pascarella, E. T. (2001). Identifying excellence in undergraduate education: Are we even close? *Change, 33*(3), 18–23.

Pascarella, E. T., & Terenzini, P. T. (1991). *How college affects students: Findings and insights from twenty years of research.* San Francisco, CA: Jossey-Bass.

Pascarella, E. T., & Terenzini, P. T. (1995). The impact of college on students: Myths, rational myths, and some other things that may not be true. *NACADA Journal, 15*(2), 26–33.

Pascarella, E. T., & Terenzini, P. T. (2005). *How college affects students: Vol. 2. A third decade of research.* San Francisco, CA: Jossey-Bass.

Pattenaude, R., & Bassis, M. (1990). The role of scholarship in serving the mission of AASCU institutions. In J. W. Bardo (Ed.), *Defining the missions of AASCU institutions* (pp. 83–94). Washington, DC: American Association of State Colleges and Universities.

Pellino, G. R., Blackburn, R. T., & Boberg, A. L. (1984). The dimensions of academic scholarship: Faculty and administrator views. *Research in Higher Education, 20*(1), 103–115.

Perry, R. P., Menec, V. H., Struthers, C. W., Hechter, F. J., Schonwetter, D. J., & Menges, R. J. (1997). Faculty in transition: A longitudinal analysis of the role of perceived control and type of institution in adjustment to postsecondary institutions. *Research in Higher Education, 38*(5), 519–556.

Perry, W. G., Jr. (1970). *Forms of intellectual and ethical development in the college years: A scheme.* New York, NY: Holt, Rinehart, & Winston.

Phillips, G. M., Gouran, D. S., Kuehn, S. A., & Wood, J. T. (1994). *Survival in the academy: A guide for beginning academics.* Cresskill, NJ: Hampton.

Pickering, S. (2004). *Letters to a teacher.* New York, NY: Atlantic Monthly.

Pitts, J. M., White, W. G., Jr., & Harrison, A. B. (1999). Student academic underpreparedness: Effects on faculty. *Review of Higher Education, 22*(4), 343–365.

Price, D. J. D. (1986). *Little science, big science—and beyond.* New York, NY: Columbia University Press.

Pruitt-Logan, A. S., & Gaff, J. G. (2004). Preparing future faculty: Changing the culture of doctoral education. In D. H. Wulff, A. E. Austin, & Associates, *Paths to the professoriate: Strategies for enriching the preparation of future faculty* (pp. 177–216). San Francisco, CA: Jossey-Bass.

Ramsden, P. (1992). *Learning to teach in higher education*. New York, NY: Routledge.

Rees, N. S. (2001). *In response*. Retrieved April 18, 2006, from the California State University–Hayward web site: http://www.csuhayward.edu/about_csuh/president/speeches_pubs/rees_pub_1_15_01.html

Rice, R. E. (2004). The future of the American faculty: An interview with Martin J. Finkelstein and Jack H. Schuster. *Change, 36*(2), 27–35.

Richlin, L. (Ed.). (1993). *New directions for teaching and learning: No. 54: Preparing faculty for the new conceptions of scholarship*. San Francisco, CA: Jossey-Bass.

Riesman, D. (1965). *Constraint and variety in American education* (2nd ed.). Lincoln, NE: University of Nebraska Press.

Robbins, S. B., Lauver, K., Le, H., Davis, D., Langley, R., & Carlstrom, A. (2004). Do psychosocial and study skill factors predict college outcomes?: A meta-analysis. *Psychological Bulletin, 130*(2), 261–288.

Roth, J. K. (Ed.). (1997). *Inspiring teaching: Carnegie professors of the year speak*. Bolton, MA: Anker.

Ruben, B. D. (Ed.). (2004). *Pursuing excellence in higher education: Eight fundamental challenges*. San Francisco, CA: Jossey-Bass.

Ruscio, K. P. (1987). The distinctive scholarship of the selective liberal arts college. *Journal of Higher Education, 58*(2), 205–222.

Russell, S. H., Cox, R. S., Williamson, C., Boismier, J., Javitz, H., Fairweather, J., & Zimbler, L. J. (1990). *Faculty in higher education institutions, 1988*. Washington, DC: U. S. Department of Education, Office of Educational Research and Improvement.

Sangren, P. V. (1931a). An arraignment of productivity. *Journal of Higher Education, 2*(2), 87–92.

Sangren, P. V. (1931b). The scholarship of faculties in American teacher's colleges and normal schools. *School and Society, 33*(854), 642–644.

Savage, W. W., Jr. (2003). Scribble, scribble toil and trouble: Forced productivity in the modern university. *Journal of Scholarly Publishing, 35*(1), 40–46.

Schaefer, W. D. (1990). *Education without compromise: From chaos to coherence in higher education.* San Francisco, CA: Jossey-Bass.

Schneider, C. G. (2005). Liberal education: Slip-sliding away? In R. H. Hersh & J. Merrow (Eds.), *Declining by degrees: Higher education at risk* (pp. 61–76). New York, NY: Palgrave Macmillan.

Schon, D. A. (1995). The new scholarship requires a new epistemology. *Change, 27*(6), 26–35.

Schoenfeld, A. C., & Magnan, R. (1994). *Mentor in a manual: Climbing the academic ladder to tenure* (2nd ed.). Madison, WI: Atwood.

Schuster, J. H. (1999). Foreword. In R. J. Menges & Associates (Eds.), *Faculty in new jobs: A guide to settling in, becoming established, and building institutional support* (pp. xi–xvi). San Francisco, CA: Jossey-Bass.

Selingo, J. (2000, November 17). Facing new missions and rivals, state colleges seek a makeover. *The Chronicle of Higher Education*, pp. A40–A42.

Silverman, F. H. (2004). *Collegiality and service for tenure and beyond: Acquiring a reputation as a team player.* Westport, CT: Praeger.

Smith, P. (1990). *Killing the spirit: Higher education in America.* New York, NY: Viking.

Solomon, R., & Solomon, J. (1993). *Up the university: Re-creating higher education in America.* Reading, MA: Addison-Wesley.

Spence, L. D. (2001). The case against teaching. *Change, 33*(6), 10–19.

Sperber, M. (2000). *Beer and circus: How big-time sports is crippling undergraduate education.* New York, NY: Henry Holt & Co.

Stack, S. (2003). Research productivity and student evaluation of teaching in social science classes: A research note. *Research in Higher Education, 44*(5), 539–556.

Sternberg, R. J., & Grigorenko, E. L. (1997). Are cognitive styles still in style? *American Psychologist, 52*(7), 700–712.

Suhrie, A. L. (1932). To what extent should faculty members be productive? In *Yearbook of the American Association of Teachers Colleges* (Vol. 11, pp. 57–61). Washington, DC: National Education Association.

Sykes, C. J. (1988). *Profscam: Professors and the demise of higher education.* Washington, DC: Regnery Gateway.

Tagg, J. (2003). *The learning paradigm college.* Bolton, MA: Anker.

Tang, T. L., & Chamberlain, M. (1997). Attitudes toward research and teaching: Differences between administrators and faculty members. *Journal of Higher Education, 68*(2), 212–227.

Tierney, W. G., & Benseman, E. M. (1996). *Promotion and tenure: Community and socialization in academe.* Albany, NY: State University of New York Press.

Tierney, W. G., & Rhoads, R. A. (1994). *Faculty socialization as a cultural process: A mirror of institutional commitment* (ASHE-ERIC Higher Education Report No. 93–6). Washington, DC: George Washington University School of Education and Human Development.

Toma, J. D. (2003). *Football U.: Spectator sports in the life of the American university.* Ann Arbor, MI: University of Michigan Press.

Tompkins, J. (1996). *A life in school: What the teacher learned.* New York, NY: Perseus Books.

Toutkoushian, R. K., Porter, S. R., Danielson, C., & Hollis, P. R. (2003). Using publications counts to measure an institution's research productivity. *Research in Higher Education, 44*(2), 121–148.

Umbach, P. D., & Wawrzynski, M. R. (2005). Faculty do matter: The role of college faculty in student learning and engagement. *Research in Higher Education, 46*(2), 153–184.

U.S. Department of Education, National Center for Education Statistics. (2003). *Number of institutions and enrollment in degree-granting institutions, by size, type and control of institution: Fall 2001.* Retrieved March 27, 2006, from: http://nces.ed.gov//programs/digest/d03/tables/pdf/table217.pdf

Van den Berghe, P. L. (1970). *Academic gamesmanship: How to make a Ph.D. pay.* New York, NY: Abelard-Schuman.

Vanderstaay, S. L. (2005, June 10). In the right direction. *The Chronicle of Higher Education,* p. B5.

Weissberg, N. C., & Owen, D. R. (2005). Do psychosocial and study skill factors predict college outcomes?: Comment on Robbins et al. *Psychological Bulletin, 131*(3), 407–409.

Wergin, J. (2002). Reflections on the faculty work project. In L. A. McMillin & W. G. Berberet (Eds.), *A new academic compact: Revisioning the relationship between faculty and their institutions* (pp. 185–198). Bolton, MA: Anker.

Wesley, E. B. (1957). *NEA: The first hundred years.* New York, NY: Harper.

Wilson, T. D., Damiani, M., & Shelton, N. (2002). Improving the academic performance of college students with brief attributional interventions. In J. Aronson (Ed.), *Improving academic achievement: Impact of psychological factors on education* (pp. 89–108). San Diego, CA: Academic Press.

Wright, M. (2005). Always at odds? Congruence in faculty beliefs about teaching at a research university. *Journal of Higher Education, 76*(3), 331–353.

Wright, M. C., Assar, N., Kain, E. L., Kramer, L., Howery, C. B., McKinney, K., Glass, B., & Atkinson, M. (2004). Greedy institutions: The importance of institutional context for teaching in higher education. *Teaching Sociology, 32*(2), 144–159.

Wulff, D. H., Austin, A. E., Nyquist, J. D., & Sprague, J. (2004). The development of graduate students as teaching scholars: A four-year longitudinal study. In D. H. Wulff, A. E. Austin, & Associates, *Paths to the professoriate: Strategies for enriching the preparation of future faculty* (pp. 46–73). San Francisco, CA: Jossey-Bass.

Zemsky, R., Wegner, G. R., & Massy, W. F. (2005). *Remaking the American university: Market-smart and mission-centered.* New Brunswick, NJ: Rutgers University Press.

Zusman, A. (2005). Issues facing higher education in the twenty-first century. In P. G. Altbach, R. O. Berdahl, & P. J. Gumport (Eds.), *American higher education in the twenty-first century: Social, political, and economic challenges* (2nd ed., pp. 109–150). Baltimore, MD: The Johns Hopkins University Press.

Index